BUILDING TEAM-BASED WORKING

A PRACTICAL GUIDE TO ORGANIZATIONAL TRANSFORMATION

To Gillian Hardy, source of elegant ideas, support, creative challenge, affirmation, and quiet, consistent strength. God only knows where I'd be without you. (MW)

To Max. (LM)

BUILDING TEAM-BASED WORKING

A PRACTICAL GUIDE TO ORGANIZATIONAL TRANSFORMATION

Michael A. West
and
Lynn Markiewicz

BPS Blackwell

350 Main Street, Malden, MA 02148-5020, USA
108 Cowley Road, Oxford OX4 1JF, UK
550 Swanston Street, Carlton, Victoria 3053, Australia

First published 2004 by The British Psychological Society
and Blackwell Publishing Ltd.

Library of Congress Cataloging-in-Publication Data
West, Michael A., 1951–
Building team-based working: a practical guide to organizational
transformation / Michael A. West and Lynn Markiewicz.
p. cm. – (One stop training)
Includes index.
ISBN 1-4051-0611-5 (hardcover : alk. paper)
1. Teams in the workplace.   I. Markiewicz, Lynn.   II. Title.
III. Series.

HD66.W47 2004
658.4′02–dc21
2003002632

A catalogue record for this title is available from the British Library.

Set in 10/12 Book Antique
by Graphicraft Limited, Hong Kong
Printed and bound in the United Kingdom
by MPG Books, Bodmin, Cornwall

For further information on
Blackwell Publishing, visit our website:
http://www.blackwellpublishing.com

CONTENTS

ACKNOWLEDGEMENTS

We are grateful to several people whose efforts and wisdom have helped to shape this book. They include Raey Currie of Grampian Enterprise, who enabled us to work with 16 organizations in the oil and gas industry in the Grampian Region developing and testing these ideas as the companies introduced team-based working; the many managers who led the initiative in their organizations in Grampian Region; Annette Brooks-Rooney, who provided crucial support for the project at its inception; Linda Hanson of Calderdale Community Health Trust, who courageously involved us in introducing team-based working in her organization, which was a great source of learning; Carol Borrill, who has done considerable work in applying and testing these ideas in organizations; and Jasmin Desai and Angie Harris, who helped to turn our ideas and experiences into a more structured and readable form. Our thanks also go to Grampian Enterprise and the Engineering Industry Training Board for their support during the early stages of the project.

1

INTRODUCTION TO TEAM-BASED ORGANIZATIONS

He makes tools (and does so within more than one technical tradition), builds shelters, takes over natural refuges by exploiting fire, and sallies out of them to hunt and gather his food. He does this in groups with a discipline that can sustain complicated operations; he therefore has some ability to exchange ideas by speech. The basic biological units of his hunting groups probably prefigure the nuclear family of man, being founded on the institutions of the home base and a sexual differentiation of activity. There may even be some complexity of social organization in so far as fire-bearers and gatherers or old creatures whose memories made them the data banks of their 'societies' could be supported by the labour of others. There has to be some social organization to permit the sharing of co-operatively obtained food, too. There is nothing to be usefully added to an account such as this by pretending to say where exactly can be found a prehistorical point or dividing line at which such things had come to be, but subsequent human history is unimaginable without them.

**J.M. Roberts (1995). *The History of the World.*
Harmondsworth, UK: Penguin, p. 18**

The activity of a group of people working cooperatively to achieve shared goals via differentiation of roles and using elaborate systems of communication is basic to our species. The current enthusiasm for team working in organizations reflects a deeper, perhaps unconscious, recognition that this way of working offers the promise of greater progress than can be achieved through individual endeavour or through mechanistic approaches to work. This is the way we have always lived, loved and worked. We have raised our young in groups, hunted wildebeest, built our cities and grown and harvested our crops, largely in groups with, as Roberts says, a discipline that can sustain the complicated process of team working.

To live, work, and play in human society is to cooperate with others. We express both our collective identity and our individuality in groups and organizations. Our common experiences of living and working together bind us with each other and with our predecessors. Today we face new demands that make cooperative work in teams more vital and more challenging. To meet the pressures of the global marketplace, organizations are moving away from rigid, hierarchical structures to more organic, flexible forms. Teams are developing and marketing products, solving production problems, and creating corporate strategy. Managers are experimenting with participation, high-commitment organizations, self-managing work teams, labour–management cooperation, and gain-sharing programmes. These innovations, though they have different backgrounds, all involve the explicit use of teams to accomplish central organizational tasks. The team rather than the individual is increasingly considered the basic building block of organizations.

Teamwork is spilling out across organizational and national boundaries. Many manufacturers form teams with suppliers to boost quality, reduce costs and assure continuous improvement. International alliances are becoming the accepted way to participate in the global marketplace. American and Japanese automakers and other traditional competitors have developed a wide variety of cooperative strategies. Increasingly, people with different organizational and national loyalties from diverse cultural backgrounds and unequal status are asked to work together. And teams from commercial organizations are linking with those from universities to develop exciting, useful and radical innovations.

In this book, we outline not so much how to build effective teams – there are many books that address this issue – but rather how to build organizations that are structured around teams. This is because, in contrast with the wealth of advice on teambuilding and teamworking, there is astonishingly little guidance or advice to managers on how to build team-based organizations. *The overall challenge is to answer the question: how can we build organizations that ensure the effectiveness of work teams and of their organizations?* This book provides a synthesis of knowledge about how to build organizations that are team-based rather than individually based, with a clear focus on the psychological and social processes and emerging relationships that can facilitate or obstruct successful teamwork across organizations. The book is based on evidence gathered by the authors over 20 years through practical management experience, research work in organizations, and consultancy experience across the public (e.g. health care), manufacturing and service sectors in helping to introduce team-based working (TBW).

The book has six main sections describing the six main stages of developing TBW in an organization. Chapters 2–7 follow a common structure. The aims and activities of each of the stages are described and then appropriate support materials and tools are provided. The CD accompanying this book provides these materials in a format in which they can be downloaded for use by managers and consultants intent on introducing TBW in their organizations.

1.1   THE SIX STAGES OF TBW

The six stages of TBW are:

1   *Deciding on TBW*: understanding the value and benefits of TBW and conducting an organizational review. Before introducing TBW it is important to understand the existing structure, culture and extent of team working in the organization. This stage also involves developing a plan for the implementation of TBW.
2   *Developing support systems*: this stage requires an examination of support systems relevant to TBW such as training, reward systems, communication, and interteam relations, and making plans to adapt or develop them for TBW.
3   *Team leader and team member selection*: establishing criteria for team leader and team member selection and implementing appropriate recruitment and selection processes. Team leader training is important – leading teams is very different from other kinds of leadership so team leaders need to be equipped with the necessary knowledge skills and attitudes.

4 *Developing effective teams*: understanding and enabling the team development process, which includes clarifying objectives, roles, communication processes and decision-making processes.
5 *Reviewing and sustaining team effectiveness*: in this stage, teams must be coached to set criteria for the evaluation of team performance and to identify required changes to improve performance.
6 *Reviewing TBW*: The final stage involves evaluating the contribution of TBW to the organization's effectiveness and making any necessary changes to ensure the continued and optimal contribution of TBW to the organization.

The six-stage model illustrated in Figure 1.1 will be used throughout the book as a route map of the journey of introducing TBW in your organization.

The introduction of TBW is a journey along which there are key milestones. These are listed in Table 1.1 along with some indication of the likely minimum time from the start date of the TBW change process by which each milestone could have been reached.

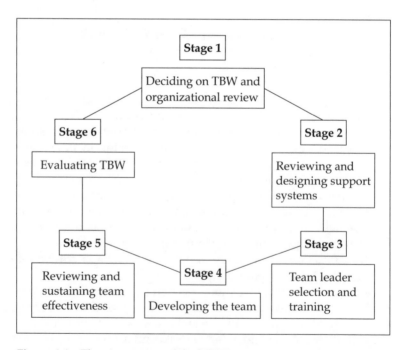

Figure 1.1   The six-stage model of TBW

Table 1.1   Key milestones in the TBW process

Target activity	Target date
Senior management commitment	1 month
Team-based working goals agreed	6 weeks
Implementation steering group appointed	6 weeks
Reviewing activity completed	2 months
New team structure designed	4 months
Support system review completed	4 months
Team leader/member selection criteria agreed	4 months
Initial team leader training completed	6 months
Team leader learning sets established	7 months
Development plans in place	7 months
Support systems changes completed	9 months
Initial team performance evaluations completed	15 months
Evaluation completed	18 months

1.2   MANAGING EXPECTATIONS AND TIMESCALES

Introducing TBW into an organization is not a 'quick fix'. The process of introducing TBW requires deep and wide-ranging changes within the organization. Achieving these changes takes time and you should expect that their initial implementation will take at least one year, and that ensuring that the changes are firmly bedded down within the organization will take at least two years. TBW requires a change of structure – for example, changing the way people work with each other, share information and make decisions – and also a change of culture. In addition, working in teams requires different knowledge, skills and attitudes. That is why many different groups within the organization will be affected by the team development process. Managers should therefore plan to involve a considerable number of staff members in this process, and not simply the top management team.

What does it mean to be the leader of this change process? It requires that the leader has a thorough knowledge in advance of the contents of all the modules, and that he or she has studied the map of the journey very carefully before embarking on the process of introducing TBW. The leader should have the backing and the confidence of the top management team in the organization. The leader of the change process will have to manage and

tolerate the conflict, resistance and pain associated with the introduction of such a major change within the organization. To achieve
this, the leader needs to have a strongly held and positive vision
of the value of the process. The leaders of the change should also
consider from where they will draw their support, and this should
include the members of the top management team.

Because the process of introducing TBW into the organization
will be challenging and complex, it is important to keep a detailed
log of progress, both to monitor the process and to enable the
change manager or leader to communicate effectively about the
process with the various groups which participate in the training
sessions. The more information that you record in this way, the
easier it will be for you to brief each of the groups which participate in the training sessions. Communication is a key part of the
process of introducing TBW and the more able you are to fully
inform those participating in training sessions as well as staff
members throughout the organization about information gathered
and decisions made, the smoother will be the journey towards
the full implementation of TBW. Moreover, should it be necessary
to involve new members of the senior management team, you
will be in a position to brief them adequately because you have
kept a comprehensive and accurate log and checklist of information during the process.

1.3   FAILURES OF TBW

At this point it is useful for you to be alerted to the main failings
in attempts to introduce effective TBW in organizations. These
are outlined below.

TEAMS WITHOUT TASKS

The only point of having a team is to get a job done, a task
completed, a set of objectives met. Building teams simply to
have teams is likely to damage organizational functioning and
encourage conflict, chronic anger and disruption of the organization. Moreover, the tasks that teams perform should be tasks that
are best performed by a team. Painting the hull of a supertanker
does not require painters to work interdependently and in close
communication over decisions. Each of those involved in the
painting simply needs to know which is his or her bit of hull.
Navigating the tanker out of a port is likely to require teamwork,

as is doing a refit on the engines. Football teams are called teams since they are required to work interdependently, to communicate constantly, to understand each other's roles, and to collectively implement a strategy in order to achieve their goals. Teams need team tasks to be of any value. This topic is addressed in detail in Chapter 5.

TEAMS WITHOUT FREEDOM AND RESPONSIBILITY

Creating teams and then failing to give them the freedom and authority to make the decisions that allow them to accomplish their tasks in the most effective way is a little like teaching someone to ride a bicycle, giving them a fancy road racing bike and then telling them they can only ride it in their bedroom. Yet in many organizations we see precisely this – teams are created but they are not given the power to make decisions, implement them and bring about radical change. Moreover, the number of layers in the organizational hierarchy barely changes. Consequently, expectations are not met and team members lose faith in the concept of teamwork other than as a comfortable idea about how we can all be supportive to each other. This is a major failing in many organizations that do not recognize that the greater danger is to give too little freedom and responsibility to teams rather than too much. We examine these issues in depth in Chapter 5.

ORGANIZATIONS DEEPLY STRUCTURED AROUND INDIVIDUAL WORK

Teams are set up in many places in the organization but all of the systems are geared towards managing individuals. This is like deciding to plant seedlings in your garden but still preparing the bed as though you were growing potatoes. The seedlings are unlikely to survive. Creating team-based organizations means radically altering the structure, the support systems and the culture. Instead of the focus being on the management of individual performance, as it is in most organizations, the focus is determinedly on the functioning of teams, and how to ensure their effectiveness. Teams look after the individuals while the organization enables the teams. These are the issues which we deal with throughout this book but it is helpful to note here that a team-based organization looks very different from a traditional hierarchical organization and that the concept of a traditional organizational chart is not relevant. The structure is more like a solar system with planets as teams that have orbits in relation to other teams and particularly in relation to the central planet that is the leadership team.

TEAM DICTATORS NOT LEADERS

Team leadership is very different from traditional supervision. Supervisors are often directive rather than facilitative and advice-giving rather than seeking. They seek to determine rather than integrate views and play a directive rather than a supportive role. The function of a leader of teams is very different – it is to ensure that the team profits optimally from its shared knowledge, experience and skill. Yet many organizations that introduce team working nominate supervisors or traditional managers as leaders rather than those with the skills and attitudes and styles that are most appropriate to team leadership.

STRONG TEAMS IN CONFLICT

Finally, even when effective teams have been developed there is a major threat to the effectiveness of TBW. If, from the very beginning, efforts, systems and processes are not put in place to ensure interteam cooperation and support, the teams can become rigidly defended silos. Cohesive effective teams may become more competitive and discriminatory in relation to other teams precisely because they have been developed so effectively. So good TBW ensures that norms of interteam cooperation are established from the beginning and reinforced throughout the process. We examine these issues in depth in Chapter 3.

Despite these failures, we see many examples internationally of successful TBW, and their success as organizations in terms of productivity, profitability, staff retention and well-being is simply and powerfully inspiring. Each offers clear reasons why organizations should embark on the journey towards TBW and ensure they foresee and skirt the obstacles we have described above.

Chapter 2 begins the TBW journey by examining basic issues about TBW before offering a diagnostic strategy for organizations and guidelines for planning the implementation of TBW.

2

DECIDING ON TEAM-BASED WORKING (TBW)

KEY AIMS

- Develop an understanding of TBW,
- Form an implementation steering group (ISG),
- Diagnose the organization's structure and culture,
- Based on this diagnosis, design a TBW implementation process.

This stage represents the embarkation point and requires a careful consideration of the state of the vessel and the clarity of commitment to the journey of the leaders before the journey is charted. It includes the initial briefing to senior managers about the TBW process. It also provides you with essential information to develop a case for TBW that is relevant to the organization's current needs, and for aligning your organization's key decision makers around the vision or goal of TBW. The outcomes of this meeting are crucial to the subsequent success of the implementation programme. Next, it is necessary to form a team to implement TBW before analysing the existing state of the organization. Finally, this stage includes developing a plan for implementing TBW in the organization.

KEY TASKS

The key tasks at this stage are to:

- Understand what TBW is and how it will help the organization achieve its goals.
- Form an implementation steering group (ISG). This will involve meeting with key decision makers and opinion leaders to:
    - gain commitment,
    - agree organization goals and associated TBW goals.
- Diagnose the structure and culture of the organization.
- Develop an implementation plan for TBW in your organization.

KEY PEOPLE

The key people who need to be involved at this stage are:

- The change manager (this may well be the CEO) and ISG,
- Senior management team,
- Representatives of existing or proposed teams and opinion leaders.

2.1   DEVELOPING AN UNDERSTANDING OF TBW

Albert Einstein said, 'Many times a day I realize how much of my own outer and inner life is built upon the labours of my fellow men, both living and dead, and how earnestly I must exert myself in order to give in return as much as I have received.'

The following material provides background and briefing material on the nature and benefits of TBW and the processes involved in its introduction, and enables the major stakeholders within the organization to be briefed. It covers what is meant by the concept 'team', the benefits of TBW, and the characteristics of a team-based organization.

WHAT IS A TEAM?

There are many terms to describe groups of people working within organizations (e.g. groups, work groups, teams) and the way they work (self-managing, self-directed, self-regulating, semi-autonomous, autonomous, self-governing or empowered teams). This can lead to confusion within organizations when TBW is being discussed and implemented. In the context of a team-based organization, the terms 'team' and 'work group' are interchangeable as long as it is clear what we mean by the term. A shared understanding of what characterizes an effective team is more important than the words you choose to use in your organization.

So what is a work team? Teams are social groups embedded in organizations, performing tasks that contribute to achieving the organization's goals. Their work affects others within or outside the organization. Team members are dependent on each other in the performance of their work to a significant extent, and they are recognized as a group by themselves and by others. They have to work interdependently and supportively to achieve the team's goals.

We use the terms 'team' to describe groups of employees which have these characteristics:

- They share objectives;
- They have the necessary authority, autonomy and resources to achieve these objectives;
- They have to work closely and interdependently to achieve these objectives;
- They have well-defined and unique roles;
- They are recognized as a team;
- They include no fewer than 3 and no more than 15 members.

What does this mean in practice? First, members of the group have shared objectives in relation to their work. Second, they have genuine autonomy and control so that they can make the necessary decisions about how to achieve their objectives without having to seek permission from senior management. They have both responsibility and accountability. This usually means budgetary control as well. Necessarily they are dependent upon, and must interact with, each other in order to achieve those shared objectives. Team members have more or less well-defined and unique roles, some of which are differentiated from one another, and they have an organizational identity as a work group with a defined organizational function (e.g. a primary healthcare team: doctors, nurses and receptionists). Finally, they are not so large that they would be defined more appropriately as an organization, which has an internal structure of vertical and horizontal relationships characterized by subgroupings. In practice, this is likely to mean that a team will be smaller than about 15 members and larger than two or perhaps three people.

There are various types of teams in organizations:

Advice and involvement teams: for example, management decision-making committees, quality control (QC) circles, staff involvement groups.

Production and service teams: for example, assembly teams; maintenance, construction, mining and commercial airline teams; departmental teams; sales and health-care teams.

Project and development teams: for example, research teams, new product development teams, software development teams.

Action and negotiation teams: for example, military combat units, surgical teams, and trade union negotiating teams.

Key dimensions on which teams differ include:

* degree of permanence,
* emphasis on skill/competence development,
* genuine autonomy and influence,
* complexity of task from routine through to strategic.

TBW organizations have a high proportion of relatively permanent teams that emphasize high levels of skill development, to which there is very considerable or complete delegation of authority, within which team members can and do perform each other's tasks when necessary, and where team members are increasingly involved in tactical and strategic decision making.

WHY TBW?

Why do people work in teams in modern organizations, and what evidence is there for their value? As organizations have grown in size and become structurally more complex, the need for groups of people to work together in coordinated ways to achieve objectives which contribute to the overall aims of the organization has become increasingly urgent. Trying to coordinate the activities of individuals in large organizations is like building a sandcastle using single grains of sand.

Here are nine reasons for implementing TBW in organizations:

- Teams are the best way to enact the strategy of many organizations, because of the need for consistency between organizational environment, strategy and structure.
- Teams enable organizations to speedily develop and deliver products and services cost effectively, while retaining high quality.
- Teams enable organizations to learn (and retain learning) more effectively.
- Cross-functional teams promote improved quality management.
- Cross-functional design teams can undertake effective process re-engineering.
- Time in production is saved if activities, formerly performed sequentially by individuals, can be performed concurrently by people working in teams.
- Innovation is promoted within team-based organizations because of cross-fertilization of ideas.
- Flat organizations can be monitored, coordinated and directed more effectively if the functional unit is the team rather than the individual.
- As organizations have grown more complex, so too have their information processing requirements; teams can integrate and link in ways individuals cannot.

Clearly, work groups are not appropriate for every task or function within an organization, but there is much evidence that the introduction of group goals leads to better performance and productivity in a variety of settings.

The key benefits of TBW therefore are:

1   *Efficiency and productivity*: Applebaum and Batt (1994) reviewed 12 large-scale surveys and 185 case studies of managerial practices. They concluded that TBW leads to improvements in organizational performance on measures both of efficiency and quality. Macy and Izumi (1993) conducted an analysis of 131 studies of organizational change and found

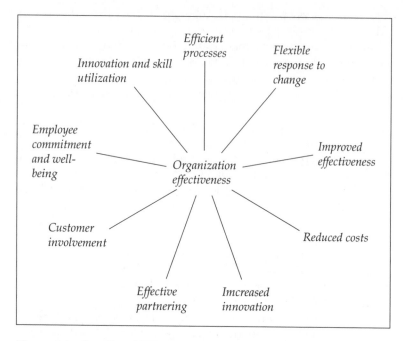

Figure 2.1   Benefits of TBW

that interventions with the largest effects upon financial measures of organizational performance were team development interventions or the creation of autonomous work groups. Significantly, change was most effective when multiple elements of change were made simultaneously in technology, human resource management systems and organizational structure, and teamworking was already present or a component of the change. West et al. (2002) have shown that the extent of teamworking in UK hospitals directly predicts levels of patient mortality.

2   *Improved effectiveness*: teams promote improved quality management. Moreover, when the functional unit is a team rather than an individual staff member, the monitoring, coordination, and direction of flat organizations is more effective.

3   *Flexible response to change*: teams make it possible to develop and deliver products and services fast and cost effectively, without any loss of quality.

4   *Improved efficiency and reduced costs*: time is saved when activities previously performed sequentially by individuals are instead carried out concurrently by a team.

5   *Customer involvement*: where teams are encouraged to work directly with customers (or even include customers in the team) there are much higher levels of mutual involvement.

6   *Staff involvement*: substantive participation leads to sustained increases in productivity, and teams effectively enable such participation.

7   *Staff commitment and well-being*: staff who work in teams report higher levels of involvement and commitment, and studies also show that they have lower stress levels than those who do not work in teams.

8   *Increased innovation*: creativity and innovation are promoted within team-based organizations through the cross-fertilization of ideas.

9   *Skill utilization*: teams enable organizations to learn (and retain learning) more effectively.

10 *Good communication*: as communication requirements become increasingly complex, teams can integrate and link more effectively than individuals.

CHARACTERISTICS OF A TEAM-BASED ORGANIZATION

Teams working within team-based organizations have more discretion and scope than those working within traditionally managed organizations. In practice, team-based organizations reflect a management philosophy that incorporates certain fundamental principles.

Team-based organizations:

- promote the development of shared objectives within the organization;
- involve all employees fully, by encouraging the exchange of ideas, views and information and increasing their influence over decisions;
- build commitment to excellence and to constructive debate;
- develop a culture supportive of creativity and innovation in the organization.

In team-based organizations, most employees are clear about and committed to the objectives of the organization as a whole. Senior management take time to communicate information to all staff about the organization's objectives, and also encourage team members and teams to influence the development of organizational objectives.

Moreover, in team-based organizations staff are fully involved. They are encouraged to contribute ideas, opinions and information to decision-making processes, and their teams have influence over decisions that are made. The organization as a whole promotes acceptance of and commitment to processes of debate about how to perform work most effectively.

Leaders within team-based organizations are committed to encouraging constructive debate within the organization. They listen carefully to the views of team members and take time to explore diverse views and differences of opinion. They also encourage the expression of minority points of view and value opportunities for careful discussion about the best ways of delivering products and services.

In team-based organizations there is necessarily a culture supportive of creativity and innovation. Teams are hothouses for creative ideas, and the organization must encourage the expression and implementation of ideas for new and improved products, processes and ways of working. If it fails to do this, both the impetus for and the value of TBW are lost.

To ensure the achievement of these aims, team-based organizations must reflect the belief that organization goals will largely be achieved, not by individuals working separately, but by groups of people who share responsibility for outcomes and who work in efficient and effective teams.

In traditional organizations, there tend to be individual command structures with various status levels representing particular points in the hierarchy. There are supervisors, managers, senior

Table 2.1 Characteristics of traditional versus team-based organizations

Traditional organizations	Team-based organizations
Individual command structures	Collective structures
Manager controls	Team self-monitors
Vertical hierarchy	Horizontal integration
Stability and uniformity	Change and flexibility
One best way to organize	Organization-specific ways of working
Managers manage	Teams self-manage

managers, assistant chief executives and so on. In team-based organizations, the structures are collective. Teams orbit around the top management team or other senior teams, both influencing and being influenced rather than being directed or directive. The gravitational force of different teams affects the performance of the teams around them. This is a flexible, fluid structure in contrast to the mechanical, hierarchical structure of traditional organizations. It looks more like a solar system than an organizational chart with lines of reporting and layers of hierarchy.

In traditional organizations, the manager monitors the performance of staff. In team-based organizations, the team monitors the performance of members within the team and the team as a whole is appraised by those it provides services and products for.

In traditional organizations, power is invested in the hierarchy. The further up the hierarchy you go, the more power you find located there. In team-based organizations, the emphasis is on integration between teams and on reducing the number of levels in the organization so that there is less vertical difference between different teams. Whereas in traditional organizations the emphasis is on maintaining power and control through the use of a clear hierarchy of command (which may be important, e.g., in an organization dealing with crises), in team-based organizations the emphasis is on achieving shared purpose, shared understanding and integration across teams.

In traditional organizations the emphasis is on stability and keeping things the same. Rules and regulations, formalization and bureaucracy encourage uniformity and control. In team-based organizations the emphasis is on encouraging innovation, change and flexibility in order that the organization can adapt appropriately to its changing environment and be innovative in its products and services.

Traditional organizations tend to adopt 'one best way' and to seek for universal models of effective organization functioning. The team-based organization emphasizes its uniqueness, adopts ways of working that are appropriate to the organization in its current circumstances, and adapts as the circumstances change.

In traditional organizations, managers manage and control, whereas in team-based organizations the teams are self-managing and take responsibility for setting their objectives and monitoring the effectiveness of their strategies and processes. Changes in the process of achieving the team-based organization are therefore deep, wide and pervasive.

So far we have considered basic issues about teams and why TBW is a valuable way to organize for effective and innovative work. Next we go on to consider how to form a team to implement TBW.

2.2   FORMING AN IMPLEMENTATION STEERING GROUP

Before moving on to the next stage of TBW, you need to appoint an implementation steering group (ISG). This should include the change leader or manager, other senior managers, opinion leaders in the organization (influential and active staff members) and representatives of existing or proposed teams from every level in the organization. The group should have about 6 to 8 members, and should aim to work effectively as a team with clear objectives, high levels of participation, a commitment to achieving its goals, and strong support for innovation.

The likely minimum period for the introduction of TBW is a year. You need to be clear with ISG members about the amount of time they will need to commit to the process and also about their personal willingness to provide organizational role models for TBW. Over that period, you may also need to add other milestones to this list.

Implementing TBW is a major innovation with all of the attendant demands and difficulties associated with innovation:

> It must be considered that there is nothing more difficult to carry out, nor more doubtful of success, nor more dangerous to handle, than to initiate a new order of things. For the reformer has enemies in all those who profit by the old order, and only luke-warm defenders in all those who would profit by the new order, this lukewarmness arising partly from fear of their adversaries, who have the laws in their favour; and partly from the incredulity of mankind, who do not truly believe in anything new until they have had the actual experience of it.   *Machiavelli, 1950, p.21*

As Machiavelli suggests, the process of implementing TBW is likely to have as fellow travellers resistance, cynicism and conflict. It needs careful planning. The innovation process is inevitably associated with psychological or interpersonal conflict. If a new way of doing things is introduced within an organization and no conflict is generated (i.e. there are no disagreements about the content or process of the innovation), or if there is no resistance by organization members to the innovation, then this innovation is not really new, nor does it offer a significant contribution to the organization. Innovation threatens the status quo and thereby produces conflict.

Managing innovation processes involves understanding the reasons why people resist change in organizations and recognizing that resistance to change is not necessarily good or bad. In some instances it is a normal and natural reaction to change. In other instances it is a reasonable reaction to an inappropriate attempt to change the status quo. Not all innovation and change is for the best; nor is it always well thought out. Resistance to change can be an important force for ensuring that change is introduced carefully.

Why, then, do people resist change?

- *Parochial self-interest.* Sometimes change is just seen as inconvenient and people resist change because it *is* change, regardless of whether they perceive it to be to the benefit or detriment of the organization. They may also feel that the change will somehow be disruptive to their own work lives.
- *Vested interests.* People resist change if they see it threatening their job security, power, status, pay differentials or the diversity of their jobs. Middle managers often resist the introduction of TBW because it appears to reduce their power and influence as teams take more responsibility for decision making. These are important reasons for resisting organizational change, and it is understandable and justified for people to resist threats to their basic job satisfaction, job characteristics and security. When introducing an innovation it is essential to think through how the proposed change will affect other people within the organization, and what their reactions are likely to be.
- *Misunderstanding.* A frequent cause of resistance to change is misunderstanding about the nature of the change and its consequences. This most often occurs when there is inadequate consultation and information sharing about the innovations to be introduced. Consequently, suspicions and misunderstandings grow and people inevitably resist or even sabotage the innovation. Managing innovation effectively means informing very fully all those affected by, or who perceive they may be affected by, the innovation being introduced.
- *Low tolerance of change.* People often resist change simply because they have endured too much over a given period of time.

Colleagues within the British National Health Service often argue that the amount of change they have experienced in recent years has been so great, so continual and so overwhelming that they feel a strong need for stability. Consequently, they will often resist change whatever its anticipated benefits.

- *The change process.* Resistance to change is often a consequence of the mismanagement of consultation, education and participation processes. If people are involved in the innovation process they are much less likely to resist the change. If it is perceived as necessary to introduce a change without any consultation or participation (perhaps because of time pressures), those involved in the innovation process should make their strategy and the reasons for this strategy sharp and clear to those affected by the change. This is likely to produce less resistance in the long run than engaging in a process of consultation for window dressing purposes only. Where people only appear to be involved in influencing decisions about change, and they repeatedly experience their contributions carrying little weight, the consultation process becomes devalued and ultimately ignored.

Organizations are not identifiable entities in their own right and are simply made up of individuals, but because of their scale and complexity they often seem like organisms, with a personality and life of their own. One way in which scholars think about organizations is as organisms seeking to survive and developing mechanisms to survive in a changing environment. Just like living organisms, they develop immune systems to fight against attacks which threaten their survival or their form. These immune systems in one sense are found in the norms and unwritten rules of the organization and can be very difficult to detect. Where they are detrimental to the organization's long-term effectiveness, these organizational defences are referred to as 'defensive routines'. As routines they are set into motion automatically and often without deliberate intent on the part of any one individual.

Defensive routines are often designed to reduce difficulty and embarrassment within organizations, and so can inhibit learning. Because they are designed to maintain the status quo, they often prevent the organization from dealing with the root causes of problems that introducing TBW might address. They are one of the most important causes of failures in the implementation of innovations, because anything which threatens to change the status quo is likely to be dealt with as a virus and dealt with accordingly. Defensive routines are so closely entwined with organizations' norms that they are undiscussable and their undiscussability is also undiscussable! Defensive routines make the unreasonable seem reasonable and are often disguised by being initiated in the names of caring and diplomacy. One example of a defensive routine is where people in an organization continually blame market conditions, political changes and economic circumstances for problems the organization is experiencing. Regardless of what goes on within the organization, problems are always explained in terms of what is occurring outside. Consequently, a kind of cohesion is maintained between people within the organization who collude together in not addressing the need for structural and cultural change.

Another example is denial of the existence of a problem. The organization might have before it the evidence of a market downturn in sales and orders, but senior managers keep dismissing this simply as a 'blip' in the market, although the blip is clearly, to any outside observer, a major precipice. Another example of this 'faking good' is an immediate reaction of crushing any suggestions for new and improved ways of doing things on the basis that it has been tried and failed elsewhere, or that it will cost too much, or that the initiator does not really understand the complexities of the situation. In some organizations, large numbers of people have survived by 'faking good' and marking time in their work. Innovation represents a threat to the cosy system they have created and is habitually resisted. Therefore, the reaction of those within such organizations is always to reject new ideas, but their reaction is undiscussable. Indeed, in such organizations innovation is often promoted verbally, but in practice any attempt to introduce innovation is sharply thwarted. Suggestions for new ideas are tolerated and the innovator is placated by lukewarm words of support but without the practical follow-through of resources, time and real commitment.

Exposing defensive routines is all the more difficult because they are so very hard to detect. People become immensely frustrated at the struggle involved in implementing a clearly sensible innovation, particularly when they are unable to understand why it is proving so difficult and why it arouses so much hostility. Below are some strategies for confronting defensive routines:

- Have arguments well thought out; reasons should be compelling, vigorous and publicly testable.

- Do not promise more than can be delivered; unrealistic promises can be seized upon to reject what is essentially a good idea.
- Be prepared to admit mistakes and then use them as a means of learning (for yourself and the organization).
- Always try to look beneath the surface. Continually ask 'why?' of those who resist the change.
- Surface and bring into the open subjects which seem to be undiscussable, despite the hostility this may generate.
- Learn to be aware of when you are involved in or colluding with defensive routines.
- Try to see through the issues of efficiency (doing things right) to the more important questions of effectiveness (doing the right things). Unfortunately it is probably when you start asking questions at this level that most resistance is met. Such resistance may be an indication that you are close to identifying a defensive routine. Exposure of the defensive routine in the long run may help the organization, even though the person who exposes it may be seen as the problem, not a seeker for solutions. Machiavelli's comment about the loneliness of the innovator is strikingly accurate.

COMPOSITION OF THE IMPLEMENTATION STEERING GROUP

The meeting to set up the ISG is aimed primarily at those occupying the most senior levels within your organization, whose commitment you need to begin the process of implementing TBW (though the ISG itself is likely to command a wider membership). Invite the most senior manager (ideally the CEO) present to introduce the session in a way that demonstrates his or her positive support for the concept of TBW. This presentation should cover:

- Clarification of key organizational goals,
- Identification of ways in which TBW will enable the achievement of specific critical success factors,
- Gaining commitment to the implementation of TBW.

In the subsequent discussion, senior management should consider who could constitute the ISG. It should include senior management team members, including the CEO; successful team leaders from within the organization; opinion leaders and other influential individuals; the HR director; and (if applicable) a consultant involved in the change process. It is important that the ISG has the power to ensure that the radical changes TBW involves can be implemented.

Once the ISG is formed, the next step involves examining the organization's objectives, existing culture and structure. A first step for the ISG is to identify what the overall goals of the organization should be and how these can be achieved through TBW. This can be accomplished by undertaking what is called a *critical success factor analysis*.

CRITICAL SUCCESS FACTORS

The primary objective of critical success factor analysis is to clarify the overall goals of the organization. As a result of applying the process the following benefits are also achieved:

- There is commitment to organization goals.
- An appropriate message about overall goals is developed for dissemination to the whole organization. Such a message is vital during periods of rapid change.
- There is improved understanding of the need for change.
- Appropriate performance criteria are identified.

BOX 2.1   CRITICAL SUCCESS FACTOR ANALYSIS

1 The first step involves identifying all possible factors – external and internal – that could influence the organization's achievement of its goals. This is achieved by conducting formal brainstorming sessions (individual brainstorming followed by sharing of ideas) in which ISG members contribute one-word descriptions of everything they believe could have an impact on achieving the goals of the organization (these are the 'dominant influences'), such as customers, staff, supplies, relationships.

2 Participants review all dominant influences and come to a consensus decision regarding their criticality.

3 They then define critical success factors. Critical success factors must begin with the words 'we need . . .' or 'we

must . . .' Examples are 'we need to achieve products superior in quality to those of our competitors'; 'we need to ensure that our staff have the skills to do their jobs properly'; 'we need to achieve effective communication of patient information between hospital departments'. There can be no prioritizing of critical success factors – something is either critical or it is not. The list of critical success factors must include everything which is necessary to achieve the final goals – they must be critical and sufficient. At this stage participants must be dissuaded from discussing 'How to . . .'. Each critical success factor must be devoted to one issue only – the word 'and' must not be included.

4   Research suggests that the most successful organizations work with seven to nine critical success factors.

Having conducted a critical success factor analysis and identified the key areas of activity and direction for the organization, the next step for the ISG is to diagnose or assess the current state of the organization.

2.3   DIAGNOSING
THE ORGANIZATION

In order to introduce TBW successfully it is important to consider whether the organization is a suitable seedbed or whether its structure and culture offer a hostile environment for the introduction of TBW. TBW requires flat structures, with a supportive, open, participative and high involvement culture. To some extent, these structures and cultures evolve with the introduction of TBW. However, in order to introduce TBW successfully, the ISG needs to know what the current context of the organization is. We therefore describe below how the ISG can assess the structure and culture of the organization.

Below are diagnostic questionnaires and guidance on how to interpret their results. These are an important part of the TBW process. They provide insights into the current conditions in your organization and the kind of TBW that will be most effective. The insights offered by the diagnostic measures provided here will help to answer the following questions:

- What kinds of teams exist already and how effectively do they work?
- What kinds of teams will be required for the tasks that have to be performed in the organization?
- What kinds of teams need to be created?
- How well do existing teams and departments cooperate with each other?
- Is the organizational culture already congruent with the requirements of TBW?
- How supportive is the climate within the organization for TBW?

ORGANIZATION STRUCTURE

In considering the structure of the organization, including the layout of the organization chart, it is important to consider the number of hierarchical levels within the organization. The simplest way of doing this is to count the number of levels from the most senior manager to the person who is lowest in the organization hierarchy, including both in the count. Where there are more than three levels in a medium-sized organization (between 100 and 1,000 employees), there may well be a case for considering reducing the number of layers during the process of introducing TBW.

One of the purposes of introducing TBW is to reduce the number of levels in the hierarchy, thereby improving communication and speed of decision making, as well as reducing the requirement for middle managers. After the implementation of TBW there should be no more than four levels in the hierarchy, and preferably even fewer. One of the functions of the review process should be to carefully examine the existing hierarchy, and the implied need for change preceding and following the implementation of TBW. Which levels could be taken out of the existing structure in order to ensure that the teams have the autonomy they need? Remember that the mistake that 95 per cent of organizations make in introducing TBW is to give the teams too little autonomy, power and control.

Another important element of the structure of the organization is the degree of integration between departments and functions. To what extent do different departments and functions interact together, share information and have influence over each other's decision making? A vital challenge in the introduction of TBW is to improve the degree of integration between departments, functions and especially between teams. Part of the review process should therefore be consideration of the degree of integration that currently exists within the organization, and the desired degree of integration and location of integration initiatives across the organization, both preceding and following the introduction of TBW. What mechanisms exist to ensure teams and departments communicate, cooperate, share best practice and innovate across boundaries? TBW is as much about bridging as it is about bonding.

TEAMWORKING REVIEW

The questionnaire below elicits information on existing groups and teams within your organization. Ask team leaders or managers to complete it for every group that you believe may be operating as a team (e.g. project/work groups, traditional teams, empowered or self-managing teams). Collate the results to inform the ISG.

TEAMWORKING REVIEW FORM

Name _____

Position _____

Which is your primary 'work team' (i.e. the one with which you spend most time working) _____

Do you work in other teams, if so which? _____

For your primary work team please answer the following questions:

How would you describe the work of your team?

Production or service delivery ☐

Project work or development ☐

Advisory ☐

Collaboration with external groups ☐

How would you describe the way in which it works?

High degree of external regulation in terms of content and process ☐

High degree of external regulation of content of work but less regulation of the processes used to achieve the work ☐

Low degree of external regulation of both content and
process □

Which other teams or departments does your work team
interact with on a regular basis? _____

_____

_____

How effective and cooperative is your team in working
with other teams or departments? _____

_____

_____

_____

This collated information will provide the ISG with a clear initial
overview of the location, types and interrelationship of teams
within the organization. It will also give an overview of the rela-
tive autonomy of the teams to determine the content of their
work and the means by which they achieve their objectives.

ORGANIZATION CULTURE

Organizations can be described in terms of their cultures – shared
meanings, values, attitudes and beliefs of members (Schein, 1992).
Surface manifestations of culture include: hierarchy, pay levels,
job descriptions, informal practices and norms, espoused values
and rituals, stories, jokes and jargon, and the physical environment. Leaders speculate about how to 'manage' culture to create
'a service culture' or 'an open culture' or 'an innovation culture',
to name but three examples. The culture of an organization
refers to the overall functioning of the organization. It is the
answer to the question 'What is it like to work here?' Culture is
therefore about the employees' perceptions of the organization –
a perception that influences their motivation and behaviour.

The introduction of TBW in the organization requires that a
number of key elements of culture are in place or are developed
in parallel. These key elements are:

* trust,
* communication,
* participation,
* support for training,
* support for teamworking.

It is important therefore, at an early stage, to diagnose or evaluate the culture of the organization. The questionnaire below enables diagnosis of important aspects of organizational culture. Where it is found wanting, the ISG must devise ways of promoting whichever elements are weak, such as improving communication, building trust and encouraging support for teamworking. Many examples of outstanding organizations are available as role models, and professional institutions, such as the Chartered Institute of Personnel and Development in the United Kingdom, regularly report on organizations that have been successful in introducing culture change embodying the principles we describe here.

This measure focuses on the dimensions of culture that have a particularly strong impact on an organization's ability to introduce TBW successfully. The results of the Organizational Culture Questionnaire provide you and your colleagues with a measure of how your employees view the climate in each of these key areas. We suggest that you administer it to between 10 and 20 per cent of employees to give you an idea of their perceptions of your organization's working environment. See CD for scoring.

ORGANIZATIONAL CULTURE QUESTIONNAIRE

Please circle the number that represents how much you agree with each statement in relation to the organization within which you work.

	Strongly disagree	Disagree	Neither agree nor disagree	Agree	Strongly agree
Trust					
1 There is a 'them' and 'us' relationship between different levels of employees	1	2	3	4	5
2 People feel confident that the company will always treat them fairly	1	2	3	4	5
3 This company is not interested in employees' welfare					

if it gets in the way of making a profit	1	2	3	4	5
4 There is a healthy relationship between employees at all levels	1	2	3	4	5

Communication

1 Enough effort is made by the organization to understand the opinions and thinking of people who work here	1	2	3	4	5
2 People are kept well informed about any change in organizational policy and the reasons behind such changes	1	2	3	4	5
3 People are often kept in the dark about what is going on in the organization	1	2	3	4	5
4 There is poor communication in this organization	1	2	3	4	5

Participation

1 Lower-level employees have a lot of influence over decisions that affect them	1	2	3	4	5
2 People feel decisions are frequently made over their heads	1	2	3	4	5
3 Changes are made without talking to the people affected by them	1	2	3	4	5
4 Management always tries to involve all employees in any changes which affect them	1	2	3	4	5

Support for training

1 People are strongly
   encouraged to
   develop their skills   1   2   3   4   5
2 This organization
   strongly believes in
   the importance of
   training   1   2   3   4   5
3 This organization
   only gives people the
   minimum training
   needed to do the job   1   2   3   4   5
4 People could do their
   jobs more effectively
   if they were given
   more training   1   2   3   4   5

Support for teamworking

1 Teamworking is seen
   here as a gimmick
   or fad   1   2   3   4   5
2 People here are
   enthusiastic about
   the idea of working
   in teams   1   2   3   4   5
3 It is 'everyone for
   themselves' in this
   organization   1   2   3   4   5
4 There is a genuine
   spirit of cooperation
   in this organization   1   2   3   4   5
5 People here do not
   believe in
   teamworking   1   2   3   4   5
6 People here prefer
   to work together
   rather than alone   1   2   3   4   5
7 There is currently
   very little enthusiasm
   for teamworking in
   this organization   1   2   3   4   5
8 People in this
   organization are
   very good at
   working in teams   1   2   3   4   5

Having examined the existing level of teamwork, and the structure and culture in the organization, the ISG can consider what changes in structure and culture are required. This forms part of the implementation plan that we now turn to.

2.4   DESIGNING AN IMPLEMENTATION PROCESS

In the face of the inevitable complexities and uncertainties in organizations' environments, within teams themselves and between the people who constitute those teams, there are no simple prescriptions for implementing effective TBW. Achieving effectiveness requires that team members reflect upon, and intelligently adapt to, their constantly changing circumstances as the teams develop. There are, however, certain areas where problems can be predicted and where effective initial design greatly improves the chances of success. In this section we describe a model of TBW, alert the reader to some of the obstacles to TBW, identify key milestones in the process and offer ways of identifying where in the organization teams should first be developed. We begin with a model that helps to identify key domains to consider in the introduction of TBW.

A MODEL FOR UNDERSTANDING TEAMWORKING

Some of the problems in the introduction of TBW result from impatience: effective TBW takes time to implement and requires multiple changes that create almost inevitable difficulties. As summarized in Figure 2.2 and outlined under the next three headings, long-term benefits can only be achieved through persistent and consistent action in each of these three key areas.

Organization context

The top management team's level of commitment towards TBW is a key factor in any organization's introduction of TBW. But the attitude towards TBW among staff generally is another powerful issue under this heading. Reward systems that focus on competition between individual staff for bonuses undermine the introduction of TBW. Similarly, information systems that are

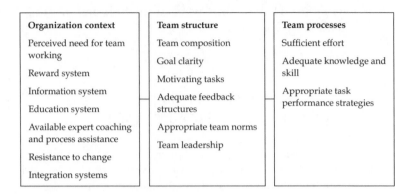

Organization context	Team structure	Team processes
Perceived need for team working	Team composition	Sufficient effort
Reward system	Goal clarity	Adequate knowledge and skill
Information system	Motivating tasks	Appropriate task performance strategies
Education system	Adequate feedback structures	
Available expert coaching and process assistance	Appropriate team norms	
Resistance to change	Team leadership	
Integration systems		

Figure 2.2   The three key areas for the introduction of TBW

characterized by secrecy rather than openness will impede the implementation of TBW. The training and education priorities of the organization must also be geared towards developing the knowledge, skills and abilities required for TBW, including leadership skills and teamworking skills. Your organization will also need access to coaching expertise to support teams both during their development and when they experience difficulties in the course of their work (such as conflicts between team members), either provided by someone within the organization or an outside consultant.

Team structure

Team structure refers to the composition of the teams, that is, who will be the team members and who, if any, will be the team leaders. This is not simply a matter of the skills required to perform the task, but also raises questions of variety in functional background and balance in demographic characteristics such as background culture, gender, age and even personality.

A key aspect of team structure is the nature of the task that the team is required to do. The goals should be clear, the task should be motivating and team members should have clear feedback on how effective their performance has been. It also refers to effective team leadership and the need to appoint team leaders who know how to lead teams and are not hierarchical, traditional supervisors. Teams also need appropriate norms for effectiveness. Teams can collude to do the minimum or not to meet customers' needs. They must therefore be encouraged to develop appropriate norms.

Team processes

When TBW is introduced, most organizations focus initially on team processes and send prospective team members on team-building workshops. Though the motive behind this is valid, namely to build cohesion, the first step in building effective teams is to ensure that team members:

- make sufficient effort (that they are motivated to perform the task),
- have adequate knowledge and skill within the team both to perform the task and to work in a team,
- have developed appropriate ways of performing their task, i.e. task performance strategies.

OBSTACLES TO TBW

As you implement TBW, there are major pitfalls in each of these three key areas that must be avoided, any of which could considerably delay or impede the process. These pitfalls can take many forms:

- The creation of teams throughout the organization, regardless of the need or the nature of the tasks;
- Setting up teams but continuing only to appraise, reward and manage individuals;
- Creating teams but neglecting to train people to function effectively within and across teams;
- Introducing TBW while leaving teams without expert assistance when problems such as major conflicts arise;
- Creating well-functioning teams but ignoring the vital need to ensure these teams communicate with each other, integrate their work and otherwise liaise effectively;
- Failing to negotiate clear and challenging team-level objectives with the teams;
- Giving the teams challenging objectives but not the authority, autonomy, training, skills and resources to meet those objectives.

To prevent making these mistakes this programme takes the change leader or manager and ISG through a series of six stages. Each is a critical stage in the process so that following the guidelines for each stage makes it much less likely that the pitfalls described above will be encountered. Each is covered by one module in this programme.

AVOIDING THE OBSTACLES:
THE SIX-STAGE MODEL

We recommend that you use the Key Milestones in the TBW Process checklist (below) alongside the Six-Stage Model (shown in Figure 1.1 on p.4), both as prompts for your initial discussions with the ISG members and to chart the TBW process in your organization. The likely *minimum* period for the introduction of TBW is a year. You need to be clear with ISG members about the amount of time they will need to commit to the process and also about the importance of their personal willingness to act as organizational role models for TBW. Over that period, you may also need to add other milestones to this list.

Key Milestones in the TBW Process

Key milestones	*Target date*	*Achieved by date*	
Senior management commitment	_____	_____	
TBW goals agreed	_____	_____	
Implementation steering group appointed	_____	_____	Stage 1
Reviewing activity (structure and culture)	_____	_____	
New team structure designed	_____	_____	
Support system review completed	_____	_____	Stage 2
Team leader/team member selection criteria agreed	_____	_____	
Initial team leader training completed	_____	_____	Stage 3
Team leader learning sets established	_____	_____	

Development plans
  in place   _____   _____   Stage 4

Systems changes
  completed   _____   _____ ⎫
Initial team performance   ⎬ Stage 5
  evaluations completed   _____   _____ ⎭

Evaluation completed   _____   _____   Stage 6

CHECKLIST FOR A TBW IMPLEMENTATION PLAN

- What is our definition of TBW?
- Are TBW practices already in place for any parts of the organization? If so, where?
- Where should we start (the senior management team, one department, one already well-functioning team, etc.)?
- How do we see the roll-out from this starting point?
- What major changes need to take place?
- What are the resource requirements?

The main task facing you and your ISG is determining what kind of teams will be most effective for your organization. We provide a list of criteria below along with further guidance in relation to each of these criteria.

CRITERIA FOR EFFECTIVE TEAM DESIGN

Purpose

- The teams' goals must be clearly defined.
- They should be inspiring, challenging and important.
- They should be discrete in order to identify this team's work from that of other teams.
- They should have clear and measurable outcomes.
- The designated task needs to be complete, allowing team members to be involved from the beginning to the end of the process.

Responsibility

The teams should have delegated responsibility for achieving their goals. This should include responsibility for designing the method of achieving those outcomes. The teams should be empowered to shape their objectives, select strategies for achieving them, determine their working methods and implement the innovations they develop.

Empowered teams

Teams rather than work groups are needed where work goals require individuals to interact closely to be successful. The teams must then have the resources, information and power to make a difference. TBW is about dramatically loosening managerial control and relying instead on leadership from the change manager and the senior team, and on leadership within the teams themselves.

Size

Teams should include only the minimum number of people needed to carry out the task effectively. However, the nature of the task may indicate optimum sizes, for example decision-making teams seem to work better with five to eight members. In general, teams are less effective when they have more than about 10 to 12 members and are not usually needed when fewer than three people are required to carry out the task. As teams get bigger they become more difficult to coordinate. It is important to recognize the need to use subgroups to manage larger teams while still maintaining the integrity of the work team itself. For example, once a team reaches a size of 15 to 20 people, subteams should be developed with their own discrete tasks that feed into the achievement of overall team objectives.

Communication requirements

When designing teams, it is also important to consider issues of physical location. Geographical restrictions on communication and meetings (such as organizations with split sites) can make it very difficult for a team to work effectively. The use of teleconferencing and computer conferencing has somewhat reduced problems in this area. However, team processes must take account of the specific needs of this type of working. Virtual teamwork is simply much more difficult and requires much more attention to the management of team processes than face-to-face teamworking.

Identity

A fundamental attribute of a team is that it is seen as a discrete entity by those both inside and outside the team. It is therefore helpful if there is an obvious reason for a group of individuals to be working together as a team. This will derive from the team task. Clear task objectives therefore determine the identity of the team. This identity can be augmented or crystallized in a team name, for example, the kitchen utensils new product development team (KU Team). Ultimately, identity will derive from the performance achieved, norms developed and culture nurtured by the team members in their collective activity.

Diversity

It is important to create teams that have enough differences among their members to produce innovation, but not so many differences that the members would never agree to work together, in which case the longer term viability of the team would be threatened.

INITIATIVE AREAS TO LEAD TBW IN THE ORGANIZATION

In any major organization change, it is helpful to demonstrate early success. One important consideration at this stage is to consider if there are particular areas of the organization where the introduction of TBW could be initiated, especially areas you consider are likely to produce successful or spectacular outcomes. In considering this issue, ISG members should be encouraged to identify areas where staff members are receptive to the idea of TBW and where there are effective leaders who use a participative style. If some degree of team working already exists within an area of likely success, then this too will clearly be an advantage.

COMMUNICATING THE TBW PROCESS

Communication is a key part of the process of introducing TBW and the more able you are to fully inform and consult staff throughout the organization about information gathered, decisions made and implementation plans, the smoother will be the journey towards the full implementation of TBW. In considering how to communicate to others in the organization during the TBW process, attention should be paid to:

- The message: what it is you wish to communicate to others in the organization about the TBW process.
- The media to be employed: this includes face-to-face discussions, team briefings, email, newsletter briefings and 'town hall meetings' where all staff are brought together to learn about major organization changes. Face-to-face meetings offer the richest means of communication since they give more information and also offer the chance of two-way communication. Repeated communication about an issue or change ensures the message gets home.
- The process: when will the communication process begin and to which groups and how will it be repeated to ensure the messages are effectively and accurately received? What mechanisms will be put in place to enable two-way communication about the process of introducing TBW?
- Enthusiasm, excitement, commitment and optimism are the hallmarks of effective communication in such a change process.

Finally, because the process of introducing TBW into an organization is challenging and complex, it is important that you keep a detailed log of progress, both to aid you in monitoring the process, and to enable you to communicate effectively about the process with the various groups which participate in the training sessions.

Completing Stage One is a major task in the process and provides detailed information for the ISG on how to begin the process of implementing TBW. Whatever the next steps, the senior management team and the ISG have undertaken a valuable exercise in reflecting on the organization's objectives, strategies, structures, processes and culture. The next stage involves determining what support systems are in place in the organization and what support systems need to be developed.

REFERENCES AND FURTHER READING

Applebaum, E., & Batt, R. (1994). *The New American Workplace*. Ithaca, NY: ILR Press.

Argyris, C. (1985). *Strategy, Change and Defensive Routines*. New York: Pitman.

Argyris, C. (1993). On the nature of actionable knowledge. *The Psychologist*, 6: 29–32.

Cohen, S.G., & Bailey, D.E. (1997). What makes teams work: Group effectiveness research from the shop floor to the executive suite. *Journal of Management*, 23, 3: 239–90.

Flood, P., MacCurtain, S., & West, M.A. (2001). *Effective Top Management Teams*. Dublin, Ireland: Blackhall Press.

Machiavelli, N. (1950). *The Prince and the Discourses* (edited by M. Lerner). New York: Random House Modern Library.

Macy, B.A. & Izumi, H. (1993). Organizational change, design and work innovation: A meta-analysis of 131 North American field studies, 1961–1991. *Research in Organizational Change and Development*, 7: 235–313.

Mohrman, S., Cohen, S., & Mohrman, L. (1995). *Designing Team Based Organizations*. London: Jossey Bass.

Schein, E.H. (1992). *Organizational Culture and Leadership* (2nd edn.). San Francisco: Jossey Bass.

Weldon, E., and Weingart, L.R. (1994). Group goals and group performance. *British Journal of Social Psychology*, 32: 307–34.

West, M.A. (1994). *Effective Teamwork*. Leicester, UK: British Psychological Society.

West, M.A., Borrill C., Dawson, J., Scully, J., Carter, M., Anelay, S., Patterson, M., Waring, J. (2002). The link between the management of employees and patient mortality in acute hospitals. *The International Journal of Human Resource Management*, 13, 8: 1299–310.

3

DEVELOPING SUPPORT SYSTEMS

KEY AIMS

- Develop support systems that meet the requirements for effective TBW:
    - appropriate human resource management systems including recruitment and selection policies,
    - team and individual performance management,
    - feedback systems,
    - reward systems,
    - training for teamworking,
    - communication systems,
    - team-process support systems;
- Describe how the different teams will work together.

KEY TASKS

- Review each support system to determine the extent to which it is focused on supporting teams as well as individuals;
- Consult with those responsible for each support system;
- Plan the changes to be made to support team-based working (TBW);
- Implement the changes.

KEY PEOPLE

- Those responsible for each support system (this will include human resources director, training manager and finance director);
- Implementation steering group (ISG);
- Senior management team.

Stage Two described in this chapter aims to provide you as change manager with the tools and materials to ensure that support services contribute to the success of the TBW process. As an aid in gathering supporting evidence this stage includes a support systems review.

There is growing evidence that the most effective TBW systems are achieved through multiple changes in the organization. That is, organization systems changes have been introduced with the aim of ensuring that the introduction of TBW and the process by which that introduction is achieved complement each other. A suitable context will support and maintain TBW when it has been established. For example, human resource management (HRM) systems must be thought about as serving and supporting teams rather than with the traditional focus on serving and supporting individuals. This is a fundamentally different way of thinking about HRM and represents a tough challenge for HR professionals.

As staff management strategies are designed to influence the way in which people behave within organizations, we suggest that you spend some time reviewing the potential impact of your current practices on the ability of the organization to introduce effective TBW into your organization. All of your organization's support systems will have an impact on the environment for TBW, including staff management, performance review, reward, recruitment and selection, education and training, communication and feedback.

In this chapter we review each of the following support systems and offer guidelines on how they can be geared to supporting TBW:

1 Human resource management,
2 Appraisal and performance review systems,

3   Reward systems,
4   Recruitment and selection systems,
5   Education and training systems,
6   Communication systems,
7   Team-process support systems,
8   Feedback systems,
9   Interteam processes.

3.1   HUMAN RESOURCE MANAGEMENT

Organizations create an ethos or atmosphere within which TBW is either nurtured and blooms in better performance and innovation, or is starved of support. Supportive and challenging environments are likely to sustain high levels of team performance and creativity, especially those which encourage risk taking and idea generation. Teams frequently have ideas for improving their workplaces, work functioning, processes, products or services. Where climates are characterized by distrust, lack of communication, personal antipathies, limited individual autonomy and unclear goals, the implementation of these ideas is inhibited. The HR function plays a key role in creating such an ethos but clearly has to be oriented strategically to supporting a team-based organization rather than an individually based organization. Members of the HR department will need to be knowledgeable about all aspects of team working, including team composition, team development, team processes, and team performance management. They will particularly need to have an understanding of interteam processes and interteam conflict in organizations and how to manage such conflict. Such knowledge should be augmented by an appreciation of what a team-based organization represents. Understanding the functioning of a team-based organization is much more than simply understanding what constitutes teamworking. Visits to team-based organizations to learn about good practice, hindrances and the processes involved in developing a team-based organization are therefore recommended.

3.2 APPRAISAL AND PERFORMANCE REVIEW SYSTEMS

TEAM PERFORMANCE REVIEW

Considerable performance benefits result from the provision of clear, constructive feedback to teams, though team members report that this area is often neglected. Individuals get feedback on performance but team performance is rarely evaluated. In a team-based organization considerable attention should be devoted to the development of performance criteria against which teams can be measured. Such TBW performance criteria need to reach further than simply evaluating team output. We suggest that you include the effectiveness criteria listed below in any set of team goals.

Team outcomes: the team's performance, be it producing parts, treating patients, or providing customer service – likely to be best defined and evaluated by the 'customers' of the teams.

Team viability: the team's sustained ability to work well together. If some team members end up refusing to work with another team member ever again, the team's performance has most probably not been functional. Team members not speaking to another is not a good prognosis for future team performance!

Team member growth and well-being: the learning, development and satisfaction of team members. In well-functioning teams, members learn from each other constantly.

Team innovation: the introduction of new and improved ways of doing things by the team. This is one of the best barometers of team functioning. Teams, almost by definition, should be fountains of creativity and innovation since they bring together individuals with diverse knowledge, orientations, skills, attitudes and experiences in a collective enterprise, thus creating the ideal conditions for creativity.

Interteam relations: cooperation with other teams and departments within the organization. Teams must not only be cohesive; they must also cooperate with other teams and departments. Otherwise team cohesion may simply reinforce the steel walls of traditional silos within the organization, undermining collective efforts to achieve organizational goals.

As with all performance-management systems, the way in which team goals are set can be a major motivating, or demotivating, factor. In keeping with the nature of TBW, goal setting works best if all team members are involved in the process. This involves these goal-setting steps:

- Develop a shared understanding among all team members of the needs of their 'customer' or 'customers' – their customer(s) may be the organization, another part of the organization or an external customer;
- Describe the overall goal or purpose of the team's activity (the team task);
- Define outcomes that will enable the achievement of the goal;
- Identify performance indicators;
- Establish measurement processes.

Teams should have the opportunity to review their performance against targets, whether set internally or by others within the organization. This enables learning to take place which will enhance future team performance. It also prompts the review of team processes that will enable the team to grow and develop.

INDIVIDUAL PERFORMANCE REVIEW

Individuals also require regular, constructive feedback about their performance if they are to grow and develop in their jobs. Team-based organizations do not replace individual performance management with team performance management. Rather, team performance reviews become the key focus which is augmented by individual performance review. Traditionally this has taken place via the annual appraisal or review interview in which the individual's superior gives feedback on the year's performance. However, as flatter structures lead to larger spans of control and each employee's contact network becomes ever wider, this is an increasingly ineffective means of giving individuals the feedback they need. Moreover, it is consistent with a TBW philosophy that the team should be the primary agent that appraises team members, rather than the individual's manager. For example, many organizations respond to the challenge of providing more appropriate TBW appraisal systems for individuals by using one of two systems: 360 degree feedback, or peer assessment or review.

360 degree feedback

Increasingly 360 degree feedback systems, previously used largely for senior management appraisal, are being used at all levels within organizations. The mechanics of the system are straight-forward: it consists of an audit of an individual's skills and performance, undertaken by collecting feedback (usually via a questionnaire) from his or her line manager and from a range of subordinates and peers. The questionnaire usually assesses performance against predetermined competencies. Answers are then analysed (sometimes by external consultants to maintain confidentiality) and feedback is given to the individual. This can be done in a team setting where the process is facilitated by a trained facilitator. The process is designed to identify any gaps in performance and to provide support in developing improve-ment plans. Organizations where 360 degree feedback systems are in place report the following benefits:

Individuals take responsibility for their own development. They are alerted to their development needs and take responsibility for them rather than relying on their supervisor or line manager.
The feedback is regarded as 'real', particularly if the organization climate is such that the system is used genuinely to improve overall performance.
When enough people give the same feedback, it is seen as true. The weight of numbers is convincing.
Individuals can have an impact. People at all levels within the organization feel that they have the opportunity to comment upon the performance of those who are responsible for organ-ization strategy via an upward feedback process.

The 360 degree feedback system is neatly in keeping with the concept of the team-based organization: it improves communica-tion processes, extends ownership and involvement, and enhances the concept of team feedback. It can also send a clear message that the organization is serious about changing the way it manages performance. However, it should not be simply an empty administrative process. It is important that the culture genuinely supports continuous improvement. Senior staff should also set an example by volunteering to take part in the system. There needs to be active support for training and development to meet gaps in skills and knowledge. And those introducing the system must be persistent, that is, enough time should be dedicated to setting up the system and, once established, it should become integral to the normal performance management system.

Peer review

Team peer review is a more informal version of the 360 degree feedback system described above. However, it may be more appropriate at team level where numbers are not so large and where the most potent feedback is from peers rather than superiors or subordinates. TBW peer review of an individual's performance achieves its effects by the following means. It reviews:

- an individual's contribution to the output of the team, measured against predetermined targets derived from the team's overall goals;
- the individual's performance in their team role;
- the team member's contributions in the areas of communication, goal setting, giving feedback to other team members, planning and coordination, collaborative problem solving, conflict resolution, innovation, and supportiveness;
- the individual's contribution to the team climate or how the team works.

There are a number of different peer review methods for TBW:

- The team leader collects team members' views on predetermined dimensions, collates the information and gives feedback to the individual;
- At the time of the team performance review, the team also discusses individual performance, sometimes with the help of a facilitator from outside of the team;
- A subgroup of the team is delegated to consider individual aspects of performance and give feedback to individuals on that area only.

Such reviews should take place regularly (at least annually) and be formally constituted since there is a danger with peer review systems that they become informal and gradually fall into disuse. As with all aspects of TBW, the key is to give discretion in the design of processes to the team itself. However, staff who have been accustomed to traditional forms of manager-led appraisal, or indeed have not been used to receiving any formal feedback at all, may take some time to feel comfortable with participative processes. More anonymous feedback from team members presented in aggregated form may be appropriate early on with the team aspiring to move towards a system where the team meets as a whole to give feedback on performance and set goals with each individual in an open, supportive and professional manner. The important principles are that the process should help individuals clarify their work objectives, help them to feel valued, respected and supported, and help them identify the means to achieve any desired personal development.

3.3   REWARD SYSTEMS

Reward processes make it possible to appraise and reward people on the basis both of the results they achieve and the extent to which their work promotes innovation, quality, teamworking and continual improvement. The way in which reward processes are evolved and managed demonstrates the organization's commitment to those values. Reward systems must therefore be open and clearly understood by all those involved. The implementation of team-based reward systems should be a careful, slow and incremental process. Quick arbitrary changes in the way people are rewarded can generate considerable discontent.

Reward systems should be considered at three levels: the individual, the team and the organization.

THE INDIVIDUAL

Here individual performance is appraised and rewarded. This can include individual rewards for contribution to teamworking where this is a specific target set for the individual. Performance-related pay can reflect individual contributions to the team's performance as rated by other team members.

THE TEAM

Here reward is related to the achievement of predetermined team goals. Reward may be distributed equally to each member of the team or it may be apportioned by senior management, by the team leader or in a manner determined by the team itself. It is important to note that where rewards are given equally to team members by an external party, this can lead to considerable resentment. Team members who do not pull their weight are seen as 'free riders' and their failures lead to resentment and demotivation among other team members. This will be exacerbated if the distribution of team rewards is achieved in ways that do not mirror the effort or contribution made by individual team members. It is important, therefore, that the reward system for the team is seen as fair by team members, and this may involve some process by which team members themselves determine the distribution of the team rewards.

THE ORGANIZATION

The performance of either the total organization or the business unit is reflected in rewards allocated to individuals or teams. Incorporating all elements (individual, team and organizational) provides a well-rounded reward system. However if the organization's aim is to introduce TBW then there must be a strong emphasis on team performance factors and as much delegation of decisions regarding team reward distribution as possible.

Reward systems to promote TBW require an organization-level commitment to delegation of power to, and consultation with, teams. The keys to successful reward systems are:

- clear, achievable but challenging targets which team members understand, agree and ideally are involved in setting;
- clear and fair means of measuring team outcomes;
- team members working interdependently to achieve team goals;
- allowing the team a considerable degree of autonomy in the way in which it manages its work;
- giving the team access to the necessary materials, skills and knowledge to achieve the task;
- defining a reward valuable enough to be worth having, and delivered soon after the achievement of the outcome.

How can organizations go about designing systems for rewarding teams while still rewarding individuals? Below we outline steps in the process, drawing on the excellent analysis of 27 team reward and recognition plans from top companies reviewed in Parker, McAdams and Zielinski (2000).

1 *Customize the plan.* Ensure the reward system is customized to your organization rather than slavishly copying a scheme introduced elsewhere. The fit of the plan to the organization is clearly important.
2 *Create many winners and few losers.* Reward systems should leave most employees feeling pleased, recognized and motivated. There should be few losers, and those there are should be clear about why they have missed out.
3 *Involve employees in the nomination of teams and individuals for awards.* Reward plans command much more credibility if employees perceive that they have influence over the decisions rather than a select and remote group of managers making the nominations and decisions.
4 *Use nonmonetary as well as monetary awards.* These can include a simple thank-you, letters of congratulations, time off with pay, a trophy, merchandise, gift certificates, a dinner for two, travel for business or on vacation. One company gives a reward of a free video rental a week for a year to employees (actually a relatively inexpensive reward).
5 *Give a few big awards and lots of small ones.* Lots of small awards given soon after a success or accomplishment have a more powerful impact than one or two large awards given to a select group of employees long after the event.
6 *Communicate.* Employees need to understand the reward plan and the reasons for it. Communication serves several purposes:
   - Education about how the measures work and what employees can do to improve performance;
   - Feedback to employees on how they are doing;
   - Message reinforcement: information about reward systems can reinforce the values of the organization – for example, performance in generating useful ideas for new and improved products or ways of working is rewarded because the organization has innovation as one of its core values;
   - Role modelling: information about successful teams that are rewarded offers role models to others.

The reward schemes should emphasize the core value of teamwork and this needs driving home repeatedly. Many managers make the mistake of assuming that employees understand the organization's core values. They need to be repeatedly affirmed and spelled out. Managers should also strive to tell employees continually how they are performing (with most information providing positive feedback) and to reinforce the messages about how the rewards link to the core values of the organization.

It also makes sense to create a smorgasbord of reward plans. Merck (a US company), for example, has an organizational level incentive that pays rewards to employees for the achievement of annual organizational targets. This is augmented by a system whereby team members nominate each other for outstanding team performance, which earns nonmonetary rewards. For high performing teams there is a quarterly stock option reward plan. Another company (ASCAP) allows all account services teams that meet their targets to receive an award that represents a percentage of the individual's base pay. In addition, there is a sales team of the year ceremony to which all teams that exceed their annual targets are invited. Although only one team wins the big award, all the other teams receive a plaque and merchandise in recognition of their achievement.

Of course, all this means that senior managers have to budget for recognition activities in advance and to make sure there is sufficient resource to ensure the systems really have an impact. That also means planning to collect, process and provide feedback on performance data. Those data must be of high quality and perceived to be reliable and valid by employees. The rewards must also be sufficiently substantial to matter to the employees, since the value of payoffs are in the eye of the beholder. Some organizations offer a variety of rewards from which employees can choose: travel passes, money, a case of wine, time off with pay, flexitime working and so on. Employees can then choose rewards that are most valuable to them.

The process of introducing reward systems in developing a team-based organization is also critical. There are six key principles:

1   Roll out the plan down through the normal line management chain. Managers must understand the plan and be able to communicate its detail effectively.
2   Keep the explanations simple even if the plans are not. How does the plan work? What can you earn? What can you do to affect your performance? What can management do to help your team achieve its targets?

3   Involve people in projects that enable them to win rewards.
    In other words, give people opportunities.
4   Communicate the plan repeatedly to all employees. They
    will forget the details so the content of the plan needs to be
    repeatedly stressed.
5   Get feedback on how it's going.
6   Do a formal evaluation that determines each plan's future
    and ensure this is related to the business strategy. If the plans
    are working there should be substantial changes in organiza-
    tional performance in the areas that matter. If there are not,
    the plans should be scrapped or amended.

3.4 RECRUITMENT AND SELECTION SYSTEMS

In team-based organizations, recruitment and selection is focused
not only on the necessary individual and technical competencies.
Account is taken also of previous experience in working in teams,
teamworking competencies and the motivation to work in teams.
It is important to note that assessing candidates against generic
team knowledge, skill and ability requirements (KSAs) has been
found to be a relatively successful selection tool, and one which
can enhance the effectiveness of teams (see Chapter 4).

Account may also need to be taken of the personality characteristics of applicants for positions since there is some evidence
that certain personality constellations are more appropriate for
particular types of teams. Teams composed of people high in
conscientiousness appear to perform to a high level. However,
teams with high levels of extraversion among their members
appear to be better at decision making than at planning and
performance tasks, probably because the warmth and optimism
associated with extraversion is important in persuading others to
accept the decisions. For decisions requiring creativity or adaptability in thinking, openness rather than conscientiousness or
extraversion are most important. HRM functions need to gather
data on which configurations of personality are most effective
for the kinds of tasks their organizational teams perform.

Another consideration is who does the recruiting and selecting.
In many team-based organizations it is common practice (and
consistent with the TBW philosophy) that team members themselves recruit and select new members. Usually they have
assistance from HR and an external participant to ensure probity

and an alternative view so that team members don't simply select clones of themselves, thereby limiting potentially valuable diversity in the team.

3.5   EDUCATION AND TRAINING SYSTEMS

The degree to which the organization provides appropriate levels of training for team members, team leaders and internal consultants working with team processes is highly influential in the successful implementation of TBW. Particularly in the early stages of a team's development, training should be made available for both team leaders and team members to enable them to design and implement appropriate team processes and to develop the skills to ensure effective long-term teamworking. This is dealt with in detail in Chapter 4.

As teams become established, a regular system of performance review should be set up to identify the further training needs, related to both job content and teamworking. Individual team leaders' training needs will, of course, vary. However, it is important that the management and skills training reflects and reinforces the team-based orientation of the organization. This may, in some organizations, require the retraining of those carrying out the training.

Both new and experienced team leaders will also benefit from the support of a mentor. This may be a manager from another level of the organization or a team leader from another team who has more or different experience of working with teams.

TEAM BUILDING

Parallel to the development of the team as a principal functional unit of organizations has come the development of a myriad of team building interventions offered by consultants, popular books and personnel specialists. However, recent reviews of the effectiveness of team building interventions have shown that, while they often have a reliable effect upon team members' attitudes to, and perceptions of, one another, there is little impact upon team task performance.

Most team building interventions focus on team relationships and cohesiveness, and are based on the mistaken assumption that improvements in cohesiveness lead to improvements in team task performance. In the few interventions which have focused primarily on task issues there does appear to be some improvement in task-related performance, though not consistently so. It is necessary to draw a clear distinction between team task processes and team social processes.

Many team building interventions are based on the expectation that a day or two of team building will lead to dramatic improvements in team functioning. It is equivalent to hoping that one session of psychotherapy will change a person's life dramatically. The evidence suggests that it is continual interaction and effort which lead to improvements in functioning rather than any 'quick fix'.

Team building interventions can be divided into five main types, each requiring a very different approach.

Team start-up

This type of team building is specific to a team which is just beginning its work and which requires clarification of its objectives, strategies, processes and roles. The beginning of a team's life has a significant influence on its later development and effectiveness, especially when crises occur. Start-up interventions can help create team ethos, determine clarity of direction and shape team working practices. They include:

- Ensuring the team has a whole and meaningful task to perform;
- Clarifying team objectives;
- Ensuring that each team member has a whole, meaningful and intrinsically interesting task to perform;
- Ensuring that team members' activities can be evaluated;
- Ensuring that team performance as a whole is monitored and that team members are given regular and clear feedback on individual *and* team performance;
- Establishing a means for regular communication and review within the team.

Regular formal reviews

Formal reviews usually take the form of 'away days' of one or two days' duration during which the team reviews objectives, roles, strategies and processes in order to maintain and promote effective functioning.

As in any other area of human activity, regular review of functioning can lead to greater awareness of strengths, skills, weaknesses and problem areas, and therefore future functioning being improved. Within work teams, regular away days are a useful way of ensuring a team's continuing effectiveness. Indeed there is much evidence that teams which take time out to review processes are more effective than those which do not.

Topics to be covered in an away day can include:

- Team successes and difficulties in the previous six-months or one-year period;
- A review of team objectives and their appropriateness;
- The roles of team members;
- Quality of team communication;
- Team interaction frequency;
- Team decision-making processes;
- Excellence in the team's work;
- Support for innovation;
- Team social support;
- Causes of team conflicts;
- Errors and near misses;
- Conflict resolution in the team;
- Support for personal growth and development.

Addressing known task-related problems

In order to deal with specific known problem issues teams sometimes take time out to define carefully the task-related problem it is confronting. Then the team develops alternative options for overcoming the problem, and action plans for implementing the selected way forward.

Identifying unknown problems

Here the intervention focuses on the diagnosis of task-related problems where the cause is not immediately obvious. For example, it might be that a piece of equipment malfunctions irregularly or that important information is not acted upon by another team, despite the fact that it is transmitted. After the agreed identification of the nature of specific problems the team goes on to use appropriate strategies to overcome them in future.

Social process interventions

Social interventions focus on interpersonal relationships, social support, team climate, support for growth and development of team members, and conflict resolution. They aim to promote a positive social climate and team member well-being. However, such interventions should be skilfully handled by those expert in conflict resolution since there is some evidence that many attempts to deal with interpersonal problems in teams often lead to the intensification rather than the resolution of those problems.

The blanket approach to team building often employed is unlikely to be effective for most teams. The first question to ask is 'What intervention is most appropriate, for which teams, and at which point in time?' Then the following checklist can be used to ensure appropriate focus for the intervention:

1 Are the objectives of the intervention clear?
2 Is the intervention appropriate for the particular issues facing the team?
3 Is the intervention appropriately timed?
4 Does the intervention attempt to cover too many areas?
5 Are means for sustaining change built into the intervention?
6 Are facilitators employed who have the knowledge and skills required to conduct team building interventions?
7 Will clear action plans emerge as a result of the team building intervention?
8 Will regular reviews be instituted as a result of the team build- ing intervention?

3.6 COMMUNICATION SYSTEMS

Effective communication systems are essential for TBW to:

- ensure clarity of purpose and team processes throughout the organization,
- constantly reinforce those purposes and processes,
- check for common understanding.

In his lectures on teamworking based on his experiences as a mountaineer, Chris Bonington describes the importance of establishing and publicizing communication systems right at the start of a project. He points out that it is difficult to renegotiate the process when you are halfway up a mountain! Within organ-izations also, it is better to establish effective communication systems before there is a problem, and to regularly review those systems to ensure that they remain effective as the organization grows and changes. Many organizations, often prompted by the Investors in People initiative, are currently carrying out com-munication audits to ensure that their systems are working effectively.

There is an increasing variety of communication media avail-able to even the smallest organization. Any form of face-to-face communication is likely to be more influential than written forms, because there will be more opportunity for checking, understand-ing and clarifying issues as they arise. The choice of media and the route which will be used to communicate information, know-ledge, norms and attitudes within organizations are influenced by a variety of important factors, as shown in Box 3.1 below.

BOX 3.1   FACTORS INFLUENCING COMMUNICATION CHOICES

The culture of the organization
For example, in a traditionally hierarchical organization major communications tend to take place by written in-struction from a senior manager to other staff. If TBW is to be successfully introduced to such an organization, changes will be needed in the communication system itself which will represent and reinforce the required changes in organ-ization culture. Team briefings and lateral as well as vertical communications will be developed.

The nature of the message to be communicated
Features of the message include its content, whether it is information, a directive, team or individual recognition, attitude, etc. Also, whether the news is good or bad may influence how an organization chooses to deliver a message (bad news is better delivered face to face).

The frequency of the communication
Routes will become established quickly for information that is transmitted frequently. It is important to check that these

---

continue to be appropriate and that familiarity with the process does not 'breed contempt' in the target audience. Teams are likely to have high levels of intrateam communication and low levels of interteam communication so it is important to develop the latter.

The skills of those who are communicating
In team-based organizations, which will typically have more open communication systems, communication skills are an essential requirement for the team leader role. Training can improve personal skills, such as presentation and influencing, and also enable team leaders to use communication systems effectively. Every member of the team, however, will require good listening skills, the ability to interpret and use nonverbal signals and a commitment to plan for effective communication.

Geographical spread and the availability of communication technology
Many organizations today rely heavily on information technology to maintain regular communication links between both individuals and teams. Modern technology provides tremendous opportunities to create truly open access to information. These opportunities, however, need to be managed effectively if individuals are not to suffer from either information overload or the increasing feelings of isolation that are reported by some employees who spend the majority of their time working remotely. You simply have to work much harder at communicating when teams are geographically spread, regardless of the sophistication of your communication technology.

3.7 TEAM-PROCESS SUPPORT SYSTEMS

Teams need help and support to establish and maintain effective teamworking processes during various stages of their development. In team-based organizations, some teams will encounter difficulties of working effectively. This may arise because of lack of clarity over objectives or about roles or, much more rarely, personality problems. It is unrealistic always to expect team members to work these difficulties through to a satisfactory conclusion. Consequently, some team-based organizations ensure there is an internal facilitator or external consultant who can provide assistance to teams that are having difficulty – in short 'process assistance' or 'process support'. Such support may be required at the following times:

- *The initial set-up stage*: both team leaders and team members may require training and support at this stage to establish appropriate working practices and to develop teamworking skills.
- *Periods of difficulty*: this may be either in the achievement of tasks, where assistance may be provided in such areas as coordination of effort or skill sharing within the team, or in resolving conflict within the team.
- *Periods of growth and development*: when team members are looking for new ways of working, external interventions can be used to challenge mind sets which have developed within the team and encourage appropriate risk taking.
- *Periods of review and evaluation*: since teams should be encouraged to regularly review both their outcomes and the way in which they work. If this does not happen it may lead to the development of an introverted or stagnant team environment.
- *The closing stages of team life*: too little attention may be given to the ending of team relationships. Appropriate closing processes can enhance team member learning which will be applied in future teams. Also team members' self-esteem and motivation will be enhanced by the celebrations and leave-takings that should naturally occur at the end of a successfully completed project. Teams may be reluctant to disband when their job is really done so this process should be speedily and sensitively enabled.

Each team should have a 'sponsor', preferably a senior and influential staff member within the organization who has a particular interest in the success of the team (this may well be the team leader). This sponsor will provide general support and access to required resources. However, specific process support can only be provided by people skilled in team facilitation who are knowledgeable about empirically based theories of teamworking. This individual does not require a detailed knowledge of the content of the team's work. For the purposes of this book we call these people team facilitators. The person must understand the role and the team(s) must be aware of the range of support the facilitator can provide.

The team facilitator may be someone from outside the organization. This is often the case where new TBW systems are being implemented and a large amount of process support is required. Alternatively organizations may establish a team of internal team facilitators. As TBW systems mature and develop, many organizations find they have the appropriate skills internally, often using successful team leaders to provide process consultancy to other teams within the organization. Such team leaders, equipped with additional facilitation and consultancy skills training, form a core resource which can be called upon by any team requiring assistance.

3.8   FEEDBACK SYSTEMS

As indicated above, feedback systems must be established which allow both individuals and teams to accurately assess their performance against targets and also to assess the impact of their working practices on others within the organization. However, within the effective TBW organization there will also be effectively functioning mechanisms to ensure that feedback travels upwards from teams and is incorporated into strategic decision making. Organizations can use various techniques to facilitate this process. The essential criteria for their success is that the organization climate encourages honest welcoming of constructive feedback as a means of improving performance and that those giving feedback see that action is taken as a result. Techniques include:

1   *Vertical review groups*: a number of individuals drawn from various levels, functions and teams within the organization and representing their peer groups meet at regular intervals to discuss key strategic issues. Such groups can also be used to ensure effective feedback between teams.
2   *Change management forums*: senior managers hold open meetings or lunches at which honest and open feedback about organizational change from teams is encouraged.
3   *Staff surveys*: questionnaires are distributed to all staff (or a random selection) on a regular (at least annual) basis. These questionnaires usually include a number of standard questions to highlight long-term trends but may also include questions about topical issues.

4 *Team reports*: teams produce regular reports that represent team members' views on how the organization is working.

3.9 INTERTEAM PROCESSES

The strengths of teamworking in organizations are the involvement of all in contributing their skills and knowledge, in good collective decision making and innovation. The fundamental weakness is the tendency of team-based organizations to be riven by intergroup competition, hostility and rivalry with likely consequent negative impacts on organizational performance overall – in short, intergroup bias.

Early research in social psychology showed how psychological group identification occurs almost immediately when people are randomly assigned to groups, with dramatic behavioural consequences of strong loyalty and in-group favouritism. The tendency of people to discriminate in favour of their own group and to discriminate against members of out-groups is pervasive. Moreover this in-group favouritism occurs spontaneously and without obvious value to the individual. Research indicates that there is no need for material advantage to the self or inferred similarity to other group members for group identification to occur. However, there is evidence that external threats lead to the creation of firmer bonds within groups while at the same time increasing the threat of rejection to deviants within the group.

Intergroup bias therefore refers to our tendency to evaluate our own membership groups ('in-groups') more positively than groups of which we are not members (the 'out-group'). Such bias includes attitudes in the form of prejudice ('when an order isn't completed properly it's always the result of the sales people not getting accurate information in the first place, not us in production'); cognitions in the form of stereotyping ('the sales department are all greedy individualists'); and behaviour (refusing to give information to the sales department about the likely date of completion of an order). At its most extreme of course, intergroup bias manifests itself as 'ethnic cleansing' and genocide.

Threats (or perceived threats) by out-groups to in-groups are therefore at the root of much anxiety and anger within organizations. The hierarchy of threat ranges from threats to the in-group's social identity (male managers being threatened by the increase in numbers of female managers in a top management team);

through threats to their goals and values (doctors perceiving hospital managers forcing them to consider resources alongside quality of patient care); position in the hierarchy (doctors perceiving managers as threatening their authority); to the group's very existence (doctors seeing nurse practitioners as a threat to their own existence). Such threats can be realistic, as in the battle between departments for scarce resources, or symbolic when values or norms are threatened.

An insidious and almost invisible source of threat is that of heightened intergroup similarity. Here the in-group is threatened as the out-group becomes more similar to it, as in the case of the conflict between psychiatrists and psychologists. The in-group, in such circumstances, will work hard to differentiate itself from the out-group.

There is a need to attempt to deal with problems of intergroup relations in organizations by directly addressing the issue at a meta level. Rather than simply dealing with conflicts between different professional groups in health care, we should try also to encourage awareness and discussion of the pervasive tendency of humans to discriminate in favour of in-group members and against out-group members. Beyond these strategies of addressing the legitimate grievances of groups in intergroup conflict and raising awareness of the phenomenon of intergroup discrimination in human social behaviour, what other strategies can be used?

INCREASING INTERGROUP CONTACT

A group-level strategy often employed to reduce intergroup bias in organizations is to increase the quantity and quality of intergroup contact, for example by having the conflicting groups meet on a regular basis. However, there is evidence that contact itself can increase bias, unless quality of contact is managed effectively. Experimental research also suggests that overcoming problems of intergroup bias when groups come into contact is *not* best achieved by having the groups work on a task together, but is better achieved by encouraging them to get to know each other on a personal level. Moreover these effects tend to generalize to other out-group members. In this light it is perhaps also not surprising that having friends who are members of the out-group also reduces bias.

RECATEGORIZATION

The most common method of recategorization is termed the 'common in-group identity' model, in which the aim is to replace subordinate ('us' and 'them') categories with superordinate ('we') categorizations. Social and health care workers in a geographical area may be encouraged to identify themselves as common members of the superordinate category of Arcadia Community and Health Action Group rather than the subordinate groups with which they currently identify. Intergroup bias is reduced because former out-group members are now recategorized as in-group members. Moreover, intergroup relations improve because individuals tend to engage in more self-disclosing interactions with, and develop more differentiated representations of, former out-group members as a consequence of their recategorization.

Such strategies are not simple fixes where categorizations are long-standing or where there are very strong categorizations, such as the long-standing tensions between midwives and junior doctors in hospitals. In that circumstance, appealing to a common superordinate group identity (we are all employees of one hospital) may be ineffective.

IDENTIFYING THE USEFULNESS OF CATEGORY DISTINCTIONS

In some circumstances groups should be encouraged to recognize and value differences between them. This can be accomplished by ensuring that when two groups cooperate, it is clear that they have separate roles that maintain their positive distinctiveness. Encouraging social services and health service workers to cooperate will be more effective if their distinct expertise is acknowledged and applied in interacting but distinct roles.

There is a danger that the development of a number of individually successful teams within an organization will lead to levels of interteam competition which could in the long term be detrimental to organization performance. The aim of the organization in establishing interteam processes is therefore to allow the development of individual team identity while ensuring that communication and feedback flows between teams. This allows teams to avoid duplication of effort, to learn from each other's experiences, and to coordinate efforts to achieve the broader goals of the organization.

OTHER STRATEGIES

Other practical techniques that can be used include:

1 *Team representatives sitting on the senior staff group*: This requires the team representatives to take on a wider organization role. They will not only represent their team's view but will be expected to consider the views of other teams when taking part in strategic decision making. Representatives also fulfil an educational role in developing the knowledge and understanding of their own team members concerning the wider organization context.

2 *Team member exchanges*: Team members can be seconded to work in other teams or visit as observers in order to increase mutual understanding and provide opportunities for individual development.

3 *Team news is publicized*: Internal organization newsletters are often a forum for providing information about both the successes of teams and teamworking processes. In one company in Scotland, teams regularly make presentations regarding their projects which are videoed and distributed to all other teams within the organization.

4 *Benchmarking*: Processes and best practices are benchmarked within the organization and also with other organizations, so that there is a sense of sharing best practice rather than competition to be the best team.

3.10   EVALUATING THE SUPPORT SYSTEMS

These nine support systems for TBW should therefore be carefully considered and evaluated in consultation with support system managers in the process of introducing TBW in organizations. However, support system managers often find this stage of the TBW process difficult and threatening.

Support system managers' concerns can arise from a number of causes, for example when:

- the system manager is not convinced of the value of TBW,

- system managers fear that processes for which they are responsible cannot be carried out effectively by self-managing
teams,
- they may fear a loss of personal power or feel that they will
not be able to influence processes effectively when authority
is delegated,
- the system manager does not feel that the work required to
change policies or systems is a priority at present ('We don't
have time for this!').

By anticipating these concerns you can present the proposals
in ways that ameliorate these anxieties. Box 3.2 also offers a diagnostic exercise to evaluate the extent to which support systems
are in place that enable the introduction of TBW. This exercise
will provide information about where and how support systems
may need to be developed to support TBW.

The aim here is to gather information from a representative
sample of those employees already working within teams or
groups within the organization, using the Support System
Questionnaire. The outcomes of this exercise play a major role
in the future stages of TBW. Distribute the following Support
Systems Questionnaire to staff, asking them to complete the form
with their own organization experiences in mind.

BOX 3.2   EVALUATING SUPPORT SYSTEMS

You need to prepare for the session by thinking through
your response to problems it may raise.

In order to gain commitment, you will need to display a
willingness to be flexible about the way in which TBW will
be introduced – particularly about timescales. In order to
handle questions effectively, you must be clear about the
boundaries within which you must work. Ask yourself, for
example:

- By how much could the timeframe extend?
- Could you work with one pilot team first?
- Would it be feasible to phase in changes to some
systems? Which are the most important for the effective
introduction of TBW?

SUPPORT SYSTEM QUESTIONNAIRE

Name of Team or Work Group .... Date: ....

The following statements describe your team's relationship with the rest of the organization. Please indicate to what extent you agree or disagree with each statement as a description of the way things are for your team.

Write a number in the blank space beside each statement, based on the following scale:

Strongly disagree	Mostly disagree	Slightly disagree	Uncertain	Slightly agree	Mostly agree	Strongly agree
1	2	3	4	5	6	7

_____ 1 The organization shows appreciation for good performance.

_____ 2 Our team relies on other teams to help us get the job done.

_____ 3 In this organization our team cannot get the assistance it needs from others.

_____ 4 We have good relationships with other teams in the organization.

_____ 5 Our team gets all the information we need to do our work.

_____ 6 Our team is given no clear work targets.

_____ 7 There is no organizational support when we have problems in our team.

_____ 8 The space and equipment we work with are inadequate.

_____ 9 Our team is told clearly what the goals are.

_____ 10 The organization provides us with good support for teamworking.

_____ 11 The team works a lot with others in the organization.

_____ 12 The organization provides this team with the resources it needs.

_____ 13 Team members do not have adequate training for their jobs.

_____ 14 The organization rewards good teamwork.

_____ 15 The team is not clear about what it is required to do and how to do it.

_____ 16   The team's manager has a participative style.
_____ 17   Teamwork is not recognized in this organization.
_____ 18   Specialists or advisers are available to help the team if there are problems.
_____ 19   Our team does not know what management requires of it.
_____ 20   Resources are often not available at the right time.
_____ 21   The team frequently works with others outside the organization.
_____ 22   The team's manager does not consult with us sufficiently.
_____ 23   We don't know what resources are available to us.
_____ 24   There is much conflict between teams in this organization.
_____ 25   The team has clear goals.
_____ 26   The team's manager provides ideas which help us to work effectively.
_____ 27   The team works independently of others.
_____ 28   Additional resources are made available when required.

Scoring and interpretation

First reverse the scores you have given on items 3, 6, 7, 8, 13, 15, 17, 19, 20, 22, 23, 24 and 27. So, if you scored item 3 as 7, change it to 1; if you scored item 3 as 6 change it to a value of 2; if you scored 5 change it to 3 and if a 4 leave it as 4; if 5 change to 3, if 6 change to 2 and if 7 change to 1. Do this reversal for each of the items listed above.

To give an overall score for the effectiveness of your organization support systems, now total the questionnaire scores from each respondent and divide by the number of returns. Compare this result with the following descriptions. Prepare a summary of your organization's results.

Scores of 4 and below on an item indicate generally ineffective levels of organization support for team working and a need for radical change. An overall score of 112 and below across all 28 items summed indicates similar problems.

Scores over 4 and under 5.5 on individual items indicate that some systems are in place that will support team working, but the organization may need to either improve the effectiveness of the systems generally or establish new systems where there is a gap. Similarly, overall scores on all 28 items summed between 113 and 154 indicate a need for improvement, although there are clear indications that some suitable systems are in place.

Scores of 5.5 and above indicate that integrated support systems exist and are perceived to work well in supporting team working. These systems need to be maintained and continue to evolve to meet changing needs within the organization. An overall score across all 28 items summed of above 155 indicates similarly integrated support systems. If you achieve an overall score of over 190 it suggests your respondents are being less than honest!

In this chapter we have considered the organizational context for TBW in relation to specific support systems available and provided a diagnostic tool to evaluate these systems within an organization. It is important that consideration be given to how these support systems can be strengthened before the wholesale introduction of teams is undertaken. We conclude this chapter by describing the case of a health care organization that introduced TBW in partnership with the authors of this book, highlighting both the benefits and some of the difficulties encountered.

CASE STUDY OF DEVELOPING TBW IN HEALTH CARE: CALDERDALE COMMUNITY HEALTH TRUST

Calderdale Community Health Care Trust (CCHCT) introduced self-managing primary health care teams in 1996. The teams largely consisted of district nurses and health visitors, who worked closely with GPs and staff in primary health care practices, although school nurses, nursing auxiliaries and support staff are also included. The system was introduced to improve working relationships between CCHCT and practice staff and to improve the delivery of primary health care services to the population it serves.

- As a starting point for this initiative a multiagency health needs assessment was carried out, followed by extensive consultations with all relevant staff groups. As a result the CCHCT decided to introduce 21 self-managing primary health care teams and to appoint team coordinators who would be responsible for leadership, their own budget, and communication with health care organization management.

- Team coordinators are paid an allowance on top of their wages and receive training and support from the CCHCT. Initially they reported directly to three service managers who provided HR, clinical and financial/budgetary support. However, three senior coordinators have recently been appointed and team coordinators now report directly to them. Coordinators also attend weekly meetings in which feedback and group discussion is encouraged, and all team members are encouraged to attend regular professional forums.

Overall teamworking has worked well and has been well-received by CCHCT and practice staff alike. In focus groups and one-to-one interviews many staff spoke enthusiastically about the initiative, and the majority regarded it as a positive improvement in relation to what had previously existed. Communications between CCHCT and practice staff had improved and we were told that the previous 'command and control' philosophy had started to give way to one in which teams had more freedom to decide how best the needs of the community could be served.

We were told that the initiative had contributed to the quality of patient care in a number of ways. It has created a climate of cooperation which has facilitated better interdepartmental and multiagency communications and practices. Teams now communicate directly with consultants working in the acute hospital and strong links have been developed with CCHCT management, GPs and practice staff. We were also told that communication with agencies such as social services has also become the norm. As a result patients now receive an integrated care package, and one consultant told us that this had helped to speed up the discharge process as there was now confidence patients would receive the support they needed when leaving hospital. There has also been a shift to community care for children with problems such as diabetes and cystic fibrosis. Additionally, teams have been able to target their budgetary resources at local health needs. For example, one team had introduced 'leg ulcer clinics'. As team members have become more focused on the needs of the community the need for specialized training has also been recognized. As a result many team members had developed their skills and qualifications in areas such as 'nurse prescribing'.

The impact of primary health care teams on wider financial targets was unclear. We were told that the initiative had not been designed as a cost-cutting exercise, but as one that was primarily targeted at improving the quality of patient care. However, there was evidence that financial resources were being used more efficiently and in a way that was driven by local health demands. Evidence from focus groups also suggested that duplication of paperwork had decreased, and open channels of communication had reduced paper correspondence, leaving staff with more time to pursue clinical duties.

There was evidence that teamworking had impacted on the quality of working life of many of the individuals that we spoke to. Individuals told us that they felt involved in decision-making processes, that they enjoyed the professional and emotional support they gained from working as part of a team, and that their job satisfaction had increased since the introduction of teamworking. Senior management also informed us that sickness and absence rates had improved dramatically since the introduction of teamworking, thus lending support to this finding.

While this initiative was positive, it was not problem-free. We were told that it had taken time for relationships between team members, and between practice and CCHCT staff to develop, and some tensions still existed. A number of individuals also told us that working as part of a small team made them feel isolated from the wider health care organization. Problems with individual team coordinators were also highlighted, a number of whom interpreted their roles as directive managers rather than coordinators. This had created tensions within several teams. The recent introduction of senior team coordinators was also viewed by a minority with some suspicion and was perceived by this minority as a move towards a more hierarchical management structure. Overall, however, positives clearly outweighed negatives.

This case study indicates some of the remarkable benefits to accrue from introducing TBW, even in the complex context of a health care organization. It also illustrates how important it is to tailor TBW to the needs and specific characteristics of the organization, rather than slavishly following one particular model or copying another organization. The importance of good support systems is clearly implicit in the account.

Once the stage of evaluating support systems is complete, the ISG can determine what changes in support systems are necessary, plan the changes and then ensure they are implemented. The next major task is for the ISG to plan how to select and train team leaders within the organization. This is the topic to which we now turn.

REFERENCES AND FURTHER READING

Anderson, N., & Herriot, P. (1994). *Assessment and Selection in Organizations: Methods and Practice for Recruitment and Appraisal*. Chichester, UK: Wiley.

Anderson, N., & Herriot, P. (eds.) (1997). *Handbook of Selection and Appraisal* (2nd edn.). Chichester, UK: Wiley.

Annett, J. (1969). *Feedback and Human Behaviour*. Harmondsworth, UK: Penguin.

Fletcher, C., & Williams, R. (1985). *Performance Appraisal and Career Development*. London: Hutchinson.

Ilgen, D.R., Fisher, C.D., & Taylor, M.S. (1979). Consequences of individual feedback on behaviour in organizations. *Journal of Applied Psychology*, 64: 349–71.

Parker, G., McAdams, J., & Zielinski, D. (2000). *Rewarding Teams: Lessons from the Trenches*. San Francisco, CA: Jossey Bass.

Pritchard, R.D., Jones, S.D., Roth, P.L., Stuebing, K.K., & Ekeberg, S.E. (1988). Effects of group feedback, goal setting, and incentives on organizational productivity. *Journal of Applied Psychology*, 73: 337–58.

Rogers, E.M., & Agarwala-Rogers, R. (eds.) (1976). *Communication in Organizations*. New York: Free Press.

Taylor, M.S., Fisher, C.D., & Ilgen, D.R. (1984). Individuals' reactions to performance feedback in organizations: A control theory perspective. In K. Rowland & J. Ferris (eds.), *Research in Personnel and Human Resources Management* (vol. 2). Greenwich, CN: JAI Press, pp. 81–124.

Williges, R.C., Johnston, W.A., & Briggs, G.E. (1966). Role of verbal communication in teamwork. *Journal of Applied Psychology*, 50: 473–8.

4

TEAM LEADER
AND TEAM
MEMBER
SELECTION

KEY AIMS

- Establish criteria for team leader and team member selection;
- Develop appropriate recruitment and selection processes;
- Select team leaders and team members;
- Provide team leaders with the necessary knowledge, skills and abilities to establish and develop effective teams.

This stage focuses on establishing criteria for team leader (particularly) and team member selection and implementing appropriate recruitment and selection processes. Leading teams is very different from other kinds of leadership and team leaders need to be equipped with the necessary knowledge, skills and abilities, so in this chapter the topic of training for team leaders is also addressed. However, our observations reveal that team leaders learn best from each other, so we recommend action learning sets to enable team leader development. In this chapter we explain how these action learning sets can be developed.

KEY TASKS

The key tasks at this stage are therefore to:

- Plan for leader and team member selection and development,
- Define appropriate criteria for the selection of team leaders,
- Train team leaders,
- Set up 'action learning sets' for team leaders,
- Select team members.

KEY PEOPLE

The key people who need to be involved at this stage are:

- The change manager and ISG,
- Senior management team,
- Those involved in the recruitment and selection of staff within the organization,
- Those who will lead teams within the organization.

4.1 IMPLEMENTATION STEERING GROUP PLANNING

At this stage, you need to run an implementation steering group (ISG) meeting to identify:

- the key criteria for team leader and team member selection;
- the organization's existing recruitment and selection policies, systems and practices, including any changes that you feel will be necessary to ensure the effective implementation of team-based working (TBW);
- the ISG's understanding of the future requirements of the organization.

The ISG sessions are useful to gain valid information from a cross-section of individuals, especially if representatives from across the organization are coopted. They perform the important function of giving those involved a deeper understanding of the nature of TBW and of the different ways in which team leaders and team members will work within the organization in the future.

It is important to choose additional ISG participants with care. Ideally, individuals who will be involved in TBW in the near future should be invited. They will see the relevance of their participation and will therefore find it easier to engage with the group. The availability of both experience and knowledge in the ISG is increased by involving a cross-section of employees. Participants can be assured that they are not expected to represent any particular constituency within the organization. The ideal size for these ISG meetings is between eight and twelve. As well as ensuring the attendance of all ISG members, you should invite to the meeting someone who is centrally involved in the recruitment and selection of staff within the organization.

At the end of this stage, the ISG will have:

- identified the knowledge, skills and abilities required of an effective team leader in the organization,
- suggested ways in which team leaders can be selected to achieve their maximum effectiveness,
- identified the knowledge, skills and abilities required in effective team members,
- suggested ways in which teams can be selected to achieve maximum effectiveness.

4.2 DEFINING APPROPRIATE CRITERIA FOR THE SELECTION OF TEAM LEADERS

Those involved in leading and managing teams need to exercise appropriate behaviours at the right times, which requires a good deal of skill, for example in timing the point at which they will intervene in a team's work in order to change direction, improve efficiency or change the structure of the team. Managing a team also requires a high level of interpersonal skill in giving clear direction, appropriate feedback and adequate support. A team leader must be an intelligent decision maker since it often involves working in situations of high ambiguity and uncertainty while making judgements about appropriate structures and processes within the team. Finally, the anxiety created by uncertainty, and the conflict created by interpersonal difficulties between team members or with team leaders, inevitably requires a good degree of emotional resilience.

Teams can play out many of the tensions and interactions which accompany family life and teams can even be seen to recapitulate the dynamics team members experienced in their families as children. Indeed there is a whole school of psychology centred on the Tavistock Institute of Human Relations which examines the extent to which work teams and organizations are characterized by the same dynamics as those which typify family life. Thus there are the tensions between dependence and independence, scapegoating and favouritism, and having one's own needs fulfilled versus satisfying the needs of others. For a manager or team leader these emotional and psychodynamic processes can create great tensions.

In this chapter, three overlapping approaches to structuring, supporting, guiding and directing team activities are explored:

1   Managing: objectives, roles and performance monitoring;
2   Coaching: managing day-to-day interactions and processes;
3   Leading: the long-term strategic view.

These three approaches to ensuring team effectiveness are necessary components of the team leader's or manager's work. Managing a team involves ensuring that objectives, team members' roles and team structures have been established and are regularly reviewed, also making certain that clear feedback about team performance is given to team members. Coaching is more to do with the facilitation and management of day-to-day team processes, involving an emphasis on listening rather than administering. Whereas managing focuses more formally on monitoring and feedback and communicating information about the wider organization, coaching is a less formal process, an internal role in which the coach listens, supports and offers advice, guidance and suggestions to team members. Finally, leading refers to the traditional notion of the leadership role, the process of making appropriate strategic interventions in order to motivate and give direction to the team. It involves ensuring that motivation remains high and that people are working as a team in a collaborative, supportive way and with a sense that the team has the ability and potency to accomplish its tasks. Leading involves vision, intuition, enthusiasm, optimism and risk management. It may also demand external confidence and even charisma.

Organizations that have recently introduced TBW emphasize the importance of selecting the right people to lead teams at the very beginning. Leaders who find it difficult to move from a directive/controlling supervisory role to one of participative leadership can cause lasting problems. Those organizations which have successfully overcome this difficulty actively encourage all members of staff to apply for team leader positions. This has begun the process of breaking down stereotypical thinking about who can lead teams, the criteria for application, and so on. In addition, these organizations provided training and support for new team leaders in the initial months of their appointment.

4.3 COMPETENCIES REQUIRED BY TEAM LEADERS

The team leader's role is to maximize the potential benefits of teamworking at the same time as minimizing the weaknesses. Articulating a shared vision or set of objectives and the strategies to achieve them is central. The role is also to ensure there is a climate of optimism and enthusiasm and that anxiety and anger are never allowed to build up in the team.

MANAGING TEAMS

In managing the team, the team leader must focus on team members' roles, team structures and goal setting. Good communication is essential to define clear, shared team objectives and to provide effective feedback on performance. The team leader also needs to be skilled in coordination, planning and monitoring: team objectives will only be achieved if tasks are allocated appropriately and carried out effectively. The key management competencies of the team leader are summarized in Box 4.1.

Setting clear shared objectives

This aspect of a team's functioning was explored in Chapter 3. The team has to ensure that a process of negotiating its objectives takes place, and this task usually falls to the leader. The leader must also ensure that there is some degree of consistency between organizational objectives and team objectives. A statement of those

BOX 4.1 TEAM LEADER MANAGEMENT COMPETENCIES

Setting clear, shared objectives

- Ensuring that objectives are negotiated with the team;
- Ensuring consistency between organization and team objectives;
- Articulating objectives that clarify its work for the team itself and for others within the organization.

Clarifying the roles of team members

- Ensuring that team members and others are aware of their role responsibilities;
- Ensuring that team members have goals that are unique, important and tied to team objectives.

Developing individual tasks

- Designing tasks that are meaningful, i.e. units of work that give opportunities for individuals to use their skills and to develop personally.

Evaluating individual contributions

- Ensuring that individual contributions to overall team objectives are formally evaluated;
- Delivering clear feedback regarding performance against objectives.

Providing feedback on team performance

- Ensuring that the team as a whole receives feedback about its effectiveness, performance and overall contribution to organization objectives;
- Gaining feedback from those affected by the team's work;
- Designing measurement systems for monitoring team performance.

Reviewing team processes, strategies and objectives

- Ensuring that the team regularly and effectively reflects upon, and appropriately modifies, its objectives, strategies and processes in order to maximize effectiveness;
- Checking that the team is doing the right things in the right way.

objectives must be laid down in a form that makes the work of the team clear both to itself and to others within the organization. At the same time a leader must shape a team task that is intrinsically interesting, because this will impact upon team motivation, commitment and effectiveness.

Changing the roles of team members

The leader must also clarify the roles of individuals in the team both for the incumbents and for other team members. The analysis of team functioning in Chapter 2 indicated how important it is for team members to have roles which are clear, unique, important and tied in to team goals.

Developing individual tasks

For effective team functioning, individual roles and tasks should be seen by the incumbents as meaningful, whole pieces of work, giving them opportunities for growth and development and the exercise of skills. In order to maintain motivation, enthusiasm and commitment, people need intrinsically interesting tasks to perform which offer them opportunities for challenge, creativity and skill development. Part of the role of a leader is to enable individuals to set goals which stretch their skills, require new learning and are essentially interesting.

Evaluating individual contributions

The leader plays a central role in enabling the formal evaluation of individual contributions to overall team objectives so that team members have clear feedback on their performance. Such feedback is usually given on an annual basis, though more frequent feedback is valuable.

Providing feedback on team performance

The leader also enables the team as a whole to receive feedback about its effectiveness, performance and overall contribution towards organizational objectives. This may involve the leader offering his or her subjective observations about the performance of the team, but should be based ideally on objective, quantitative and qualitative data wherever possible. It may also involve seeking feedback from those affected by the team's work. For example, in a primary health care team, the manager might seek feedback in one of various forms: patient satisfaction surveys with the practice, patient satisfaction surveys with clinical interviews, feedback from relatives and carers on the supportiveness of the practice, feedback from local hospitals on the efficiency of the practice, or feedback from Social Services.

By fulfilling the role of gathering objective feedback, the leader provides the team with information about areas in which it is achieving its required targets and areas in which any discrepancies exist. The leader can then work with the team to set new standards and devise new procedures for achieving them. Too often teams are managed as though the individuals were simply working alone and performance feedback is given only at the individual level. Leaders can contribute enormously to the promotion of effective team work and synergy by ensuring that frequent and clear feedback on performance is given to the team as a whole.

Reviewing group processes, strategies and objectives

There is growing evidence that a major contributor to effective team performance is 'task reflexivity'. Task reflexivity is the extent to which a team openly and actively reflects upon and appropriately modifies its objectives, strategies and processes in order to maximize effectiveness. In other words, teams should regularly take time out to review the methods, objectives and procedures they are using and modify them as appropriate.

Chris Argyris, an American organizational psychologist, has coined the term 'double loop learning' (Argyris, 1991) to describe the difference between how teams and organizations assess whether they are doing things right, versus whether they are doing the right things. Argyris argues that many organizations only consider how efficient they are, that is, whether they are doing things right. For example, a manufacturer of metal springs might be spending more and more time focusing on whether the correct amount of tension exists within the springs that are being produced in order to achieve a bigger market. This is focusing on doing things right. However, double loop learning involves going a step beyond and asking whether the organization or team is doing the right thing. For example, it may be that the production of springs is not the right thing to be doing in a highly competitive market and that the manufacturer should change over to the production of nuts and bolts. In relation to health care, many teams might focus on how they can improve the quality of medical care given to patients who visit the surgery with complaints. However, an example of double loop learning is deciding to change the emphasis to health promotion rather than cure as a way of dealing with local health problems.

So, too, a leader can ensure that there is a high degree of double loop learning or reflexivity within a team by setting up regular reviews of team objectives, methods, structures and processes. As a minimum, in complex decision-making teams, reviews should take place at least every six months where the group discusses successes over the previous period, the difficulties encountered, as well as the failures of the team.

It is usually the responsibility of the team leader to set up 'time out' from the team's daily work to enable these review processes to take place. While some doubt the wisdom of taking time out from a team's busy work to conduct such reviews, there is strong evidence that teams which do this are far more effective than those which do not. Often in our work with the management teams of hospitals in the UK, we have found that teams under most pressure are those which are working least effectively and which are consequently least prepared to take time out to review their strategies and processes. It is as though they are running so fast on a treadmill, they are not aware of the opportunities that stepping off affords them, either to go in a different direction or to travel not on a treadmill but on an escalator!

COACHING TEAMS

Coaching means helping a team to achieve its objectives and its potential by giving frequent and specific support, encouragement, guidance and feedback. It is the process of facilitating the individual and collective efforts of members of a team. The team leader can perform this role in addition to the roles of managing and leading. The concept of coaching is based on the idea that there should be a mix of guidance in appropriate directions, along with creating the conditions within which team members can discover for themselves ways of improving work performance. Traditionally the former approach has tended to dominate among team managers and leaders, but increasingly evidence from within organizational and educational psychology suggests that the latter approach is more constructive.

The team leader needs to develop coaching skills if the team is to evolve into an empowered team which will take increasing responsibility for its own performance and management. This involves the provision of guidance and support to team members in areas of both task performance and team processes. The team leader needs to create a team environment in which team members can discover ways of improving performance. The key coaching competencies of the team leader are summarized and expanded in Box 4.2.

BOX 4.2   TEAM LEADER COACHING COMPETENCIES

Listening

- Active listening: giving active attention and interpreting what is being said;
- Open listening: suspending judgement until the person has had the opportunity to explore the issue thoroughly;
- Drawing out: asking open questions to encourage the person to talk about their ideas, feelings and aspirations;
- Reflective listening: summarizing or restating your understanding of what the team member has said.

Recognizing and revealing feelings

- Exploring and clarifying the feelings of team members;
- Feeling comfortable about revealing one's own feelings as a member of the team;
- Dealing with those feelings in an appropriate way and at the right times.

Giving feedback

- Telling team members about your observations of their behaviour and the consequences of their behaviour;
- Ensuring that feedback is specific, focused, and aimed at consolidating and improving performance within the team.

Agreeing goals

- Working with individuals and the team to establish direction and goals;
- Ensuring that goals are specific, measurable, achievable, relevant and time-bound.

Listening

Listening is the principal skill of team coaching.

Active listening means putting effort into the listening process. All too often, when meeting with team members, the leader can be nodding, looking interested and concerned, but actually be far away thinking about a previous meeting or, say, a conversation with her daughter. Active listening means giving active attention to the team member you are with here and now, as well as interpreting what they are saying, that is, listening between the words.

Open listening is listening with an open mind; suspending judgement to let the individual work through an idea. The team coach should not assume that he or she knows the answer before the person has told their story. Listening with an open mind involves suspending judgement until the person has had an opportunity to explore the issue thoroughly or to explain the issue fully to the team coach.

The best strategy for problem solving is to spend most of the time clarifying the problem before trying to generate solutions. It is clearly not a productive course of action to generate solutions to the wrong problems! *The team coach should therefore encourage team members to explore problems fully rather than offering solutions.* This is very important and hard to practise in reality. For example, in working with hundreds of team managers across Europe who have role-played team coaching, we have found the major challenge they experience is with the temptation to solve problems quickly. Coaching involves avoiding offering solutions to a problem that the coach has defined; rather it requires waiting until team members have clarified for themselves what the nature of the problem might be. It is not the role of a coach to offer solutions. It may be appropriate in certain leadership situations but it is not part of the coaching model.

A major part of listening involves *drawing out*, that is, encouraging the individual to talk about his or her ideas, feelings and aspirations. This is helped considerably by asking what psychologists call 'open' questions, such as 'Why?', 'How?' and 'Who?' The purpose is to enable people to elaborate and articulate their own exploration of a particular problem or issue which they are consulting the coach about. Closed questions are characterized by whether 'yes' and 'no' answers can be given in response to them, such as: 'Is spending too much time at work causing you problems at home in your relationship with your partner?' An appropriate open question in that situation might be: 'How is your current workload causing problems for you?' Again, most aspiring team coaches too readily identify the nature of the problem in their questioning. When a team member tells the coach that he is spending too much time at work, the coach may make the mistake of asking what appears to be an open question, but is in fact a closed and leading question such as: 'Why are you having difficulties prioritizing your work?' What a more effective team coach could ask is: 'Why do you think this is happening?' 'What sorts of pressures do you feel you are currently under?' 'How do you feel about it?'

Reflective listening involves restating your understanding of what a team member has said to you. Essentially it involves summarizing their previous statements, for example: 'So you're saying despite enjoying your work, you feel you want to have more freedom to define and pursue new projects on your own?' Again, this interpretation should not be the team coach's own definition of the nature of the problem, it should be a genuine attempt to restate and summarize the information given by the team member. This is a very powerful form of coaching behaviour which enables the individual to explore particular issues in his or her team work more thoroughly. Reflective listening is powerful for the following reasons:

- It ensures that the team coach has to listen actively to what the team member is saying;
- It communicates to the team member a genuine desire by the team coach to understand what he or she is saying;
- It gives the team member the opportunity to correct misunderstandings on the part of the team coach;
- It enables the team coach to be confident that he or she has a correct understanding of what the team member is saying;
- It builds mutual empathy and understanding.

Some team coaches may be concerned that simply restating information offered by the team member will appear to be an empty, parrot-like process. However, research on interaction processes has demonstrated that such summarizing statements normally encourage the team member to elaborate further on the information already given, rather than simply affirming the correctness of what was said. Exploration is facilitated rather than curtailed by reflective listening.

Recognizing and revealing feelings

If a team coach is to facilitate team members' work and experiences, it is very important that the whole person is encompassed and not just those elements which are perceived as comfortable to deal with. It is sometimes appropriate and necessary to spend time exploring and clarifying the feelings of team members if a team coach is to perform his or her task effectively. This also demands revealing one's own feelings and being comfortable and clear about doing that. Team coaches may be the object of frustration or anger or, alternatively, may feel frustrated and angry with team members themselves. Dealing with those feelings in an appropriate way, and at the right times, is an important part of the coaching process, especially when they interfere with effective team task performance.

What is not being suggested here is that team coaches should explore every nuance of team members' emotional reactions and frustrations. Where there are major 'feelings' issues team members should be given an opportunity to express and explore those feelings. Team members who are feeling overloaded and frustrated with their colleagues may need some space to express that frustration before they are able to analyse the balance of tasks and priorities currently facing them. It is often the case that by focusing on feelings the facts emerge, whereas when the focus is on facts the feelings remain hidden and unexpressed. The expression of such emotions has a useful impact not just on people's immediate well-being but also on their ability to deal with similar stresses in the future.

Giving feedback

'Feedback' is a word like 'participation' – widely used in organizations but often misunderstood and rarely practised. Feedback involves giving clear reactions to specific behaviours in a sensitive and constructive way.

Giving feedback as a team coach involves telling people about your observations of their behaviour and your observations of the consequences of their behaviour. For example: 'I noticed that you stopped the group from reaching agreement about the inclusion of that set of questions in the questionnaire because you had a sense that they were not appropriate. This was in the face of some frustration from other team members. However, the consequence was that a much better set of questions was achieved and will provide us with more useful information as a result.'

In this instance, feedback focuses on a particular example of behaviour and the positive consequences of it. Feedback is not about patting people on the head and giving them 'smiley faces'. That can be merely patronizing and implies the team coach has a parental type of power over the individual. Rather, feedback should be aimed at consolidating and improving performance within the team.

Feedback is most effective in changing and strengthening behaviour when it follows immediately after the behaviour. However, within organizations feedback is often withheld until the annual appraisal meeting. This has very limited impact on behaviour. The team coach should provide feedback for team members on a daily basis.

Positive feedback is much more effective in changing behaviour than negative feedback. It is better to ensure a very strong balance of positive against negative feedback. However, because we are quicker to recognize the discrepancies between actual and desired behaviour in the workplace, the balance is often inappropriately in favour of negative feedback. This is a consequence of our normal reaction to our environment. We tend to see discrepancy when what we expect and what actually occurs do not match. Consequently the team coach has to work hard to find examples of consistency – when there is a match between expectations and reality – rather than discrepancy, and then to provide feedback as a result.

Agreeing goals

It is the superordinate task of a team leader, manager, or coach to help set direction and goals. It is a fundamental principle of work behaviour that goal setting has a powerful influence on performance. The role of the facilitator or coach in working with team members therefore must involve helping them to agree goals. If, for example, a team member is concerned about workload, part of the coaching should be to facilitate a shared agreement about goals between that team member and the coach. This may well involve setting goals for the team coach as well. These goals should be specific, measurable, achievable, relevant to the issue raised and time-based. Finally, and of equal importance, the team member and coach should take action to ensure that the goals are achieved.

LEADING TEAMS

Effective leaders see long-term goals clearly and are able to interpret their vision in a way that motivates the team. Intuition, judgement and the ability to assess and manage risk, while giving the team confidence and enthusing team members, are the main requirements in this role. In contrast to managing and coaching, leading is a long-term strategic approach to managing a team. Leading refers to the less mechanical, perhaps more intuitive, skills necessary for a team to find direction, synergy and success, and it is to an examination of these skills that we now turn.

Over the last 15 years, Richard Hackman of Harvard University has studied a variety of team types including surgical teams, orchestras, cockpit teams, basketball teams and banking teams. His results (Hackman, 2002) suggest that there are three main functions of a team leader:

1 *Creating favourable performance conditions for the team*
   • Ensuring that the team task is well-defined;
   • Ensuring that the team has adequate organizational resources and clear boundaries;
   • Using resources and authority or exercising influence within the organization to ensure a favourable environment for team performance.
2 *Building and maintaining the team as a performing unit*
   • Ensuring that the team has an appropriate mix of skills and abilities, while not being so large that it cannot perform efficiently;
   • Developing processes that enable the team to perform efficiently.
3 *Coaching and supporting the team*
   • Making appropriate and timely interventions on a day-to-day basis to help the team achieve its task;
   • Demonstrating sensitivity to patterns of interactions and processes of performance within the team;
   • Focusing on long-term individual and team growth and development.

Another view of the relationship between traditional and team-centred leadership is offered in Table 4.1.

Particularly in the early stages of a team's development, training should be made available for team leaders to enable them to

Table 4.1 Traditional and team-centred leadership

Basis for comparison	Traditional leader	Team-centred leader
Responsibility for group	Leader	Shared
Control over final choice	Leader	Group
Leader position power	Emphasized	De-emphazised
Leader perception of group	Individuals	Collective entity
Task-oriented functions	Leader	Shared
Group maintenance	Not systematic	Emphasized, shared with group
Socioemotional processes	Ignored	Observed closely by leader
Expressing needs, feelings	Discouraged	Encouraged, discussed

design and implement appropriate team processes and to develop the skills needed for effective team leading.

Team leaders need to be skilled in responding appropriately to meet the needs of their teams, that is, to be more or less directive in supporting a team. Their aim should always be to move as quickly as possible away from being directive and towards developing the team to be autonomous. When supported by a team leader who provides an autonomous environment, a team can achieve most by becoming self-directing in its development and its work as task-related and teamworking skills develop.

John Heron (1989) has identified three modes of facilitation which can be used in working with teams:

1   *Directive mode*: When working with the team, the leader will take responsibility and make decisions for the team, for example about the type of training which is required or about the timing of meetings. The team leader will also make decisions about how the team will work and interact during sessions.
2   *Cooperative mode*: The leader will share decision making with the team. The leader's view may still be the most influential but there is a clear intention to enable the team to become more self-directing and to negotiate the required outcomes from team sessions.
3   *Autonomous mode*: The team is self-directing and responsible for negotiating its own objectives and managing its own processes, including recruitment and selection. It largely reports to (rather than being directed by) a senior manager.

4.4   TEAM LEADER TRAINING

As teams become established, team leaders' performance reviews will identify further training needs related to both job content and teamworking, for example to develop skills required by the team such as financial management or information technology. Successful TBW demands that resources are available to meet these needs.

Often organizations provide new team leaders with one or two days' initial off-the-job training and then adopt an attitude of 'Let them get on with it'. Training is more productive when:

- it is relevant to the individual's needs,
- it takes place when the content can be immediately applied,
- it is provided in a supportive atmosphere where experiences can be reviewed and built upon.

The training needs commonly identified by new team leaders are listed in Box 4.3.

BOX 4.3   TRAINING NEEDS

The introduction of change
Team leaders need to be confident in their role as agents of change both within the team and within the organization. They need to develop a clear vision of the future and the ability to establish processes which will gain team members' commitment to achieving change. Awareness of potential reactions to the introduction of change is important for the planning process.

Facilitation skills
From their very first contact with their team, new team leaders need to demonstrate that they intend to develop a facilitative style of leadership which allows participative decision making and shared responsibility. This may be a new way of working for both the leader and the team. It is therefore essential to provide early support and help with processes and skills to achieve this way of working and to explore any resulting problems in the team.

Coaching skills

Team leaders must be skilled in identifying problems that may both prevent the achievement of the task and also delay the development of effective team processes. In response to obvious gaps in knowledge or skill, the team leader must be able to identify the most appropriate means of providing feedback, support and guidance to individuals and to the team as a whole. The team leader must also be able to identify the resources needed by the team to achieve its goals and how to gain access to them.

Conflict resolution

Team conflict can be a source of quality and creativity if managed well but can destroy a team if managed badly. Team leaders need to develop skills in promoting constructive controversy while identifying situations where destructive interpersonal conflict will inhibit the effectiveness of the team.

Setting objectives

Whether new team leaders are setting a new direction or task for the team or have inherited an existing project or workload, they must be able to clearly define the vision, mission and goals of the team. This will lead to the formation of action plans for the achievement of the team's goals. The process by which this is achieved sets the tone for the way in which the team will work together; it is therefore a powerful element in the development of the team as a working unit.

Individual objectives will ideally be agreed by the team in relation to the overall action plan. Team leaders need the skills to manage this process and to ensure that all objectives are specific, measurable, achievable, relevant and time-bound.

Team leaders are also usually on the interface to other teams and to the organization generally. They therefore need knowledge of, and involvement in, the wider organization goal-setting process.

Support for team member growth

Team leaders need to establish planning processes for growth and development within the team. The resulting action plans will support individual members' skill development – both in technical and team processes areas – and enable personal growth through job satisfaction and appropriate balancing of work and personal life. Team leaders are usually best placed to access the information and resources that are required to support the team's training and development plans.

Promoting innovation
The development of teams in organizations is largely in response to an increasing need for innovation. Team leaders therefore need to create an environment in which new ideas can be generated and innovations can be implemented. This requires the development of a shared vision within the team, a team climate in which levels of participation are consistently high, a genuine commitment to excellence in team outcomes and processes, and positive support for innovation both from inside the team and from the organization generally.

Individual team leader training requirements will, of course, vary. More experienced staff who have successfully used command and control models to manage performance to date may need as much, if not more, support in changing their approach as those new team leaders who have received no training in people management. However, it is vitally important that all management and skills models used within the training environment reflect and reinforce the team-based orientation of the organization. Continuing to use purely task-oriented, directive models of management in the organization's 'Introduction to Leadership' course is unlikely to hasten the implementation of TBW. We therefore suggest the use of the action learning set approach for the training and development of team leaders.

4.5   SETTING UP ACTION LEARNING SETS FOR TEAM LEADERS

This section provides an introduction to using action learning sets within the context of introducing TBW into your organization. In a recent review of leadership learning sets we found that learning set members reported the following benefits from using the action learning model for development:

The process:

- values everyone's experience and knowledge,
- is democratic,
- stresses questioning – of everything,
- focuses on listening – to everyone,
- insists on action – so it brings about real change in ways of working,
- provides support for individuals in the implementation of change,
- encourages individual and team responsibility.

While providing individual development the action learning process therefore models the type of working practices which are necessary within self-directing or autonomous teams.

The role of the learning set will be to provide a forum in which learning objectives can be clarified, opportunities for learning can be identified and the application of learning can be reviewed. The primary purpose of the learning set remains to instigate and review learning *experience*. However, you may choose, additionally, to use learning set meetings to provide input sessions on relevant topics or to provide updates about the implementation process. Ideally all team leaders, new and experienced, should be involved in a learning set – in this way the process will provide a way of monitoring the implementation process at the team level and also the means to develop and adjust the programme as necessary. Learning sets also provide an invaluable vehicle for communicating data about the implementation programme and for establishing new cultural norms.

UNDERLYING PRINCIPLES OF ACTION LEARNING

Reg Revans, the originator of the action learning approach for development in organizations, designed action learning sets to accommodate certain principles:

- Learning is about change. Learning is achieved when a new skill, behaviour or attitude has been transferred to a real life situation – and has been proved to work.
- Mature people learn best when they are directly involved in real problems to which answers are not readily available.

- Within problem situations people learn best when they ask questions and seek not answers but understanding.
- People learn only when they want to learn – ultimately the motivation has to come from within.
- Learning is a social process – in solving together some problem of common interest, learners help each other, not only to resolve the shared problem but to gain individual personal development which can be used in other situations.

The form of each set meeting therefore will allow for each set member to:

- Reflect upon their experience in relation to a specific issue – e.g. the development of a common team vision.
- Identify new ways in which the issue could be addressed – it is essential at this stage that colleagues help the set member to identify as many realistic options as possible.
- Select and commit to action in relation to the issue – the set member will be expected to report back on progress and learning resulting from the action(s) at the next set meeting.

ESTABLISHING ACTION LEARNING SETS

In our experience learning sets in this context work best when there are between five and eight learning set members (team leaders in this case) who are able to meet on a regular basis during the implementation period. Team leaders new to participation in a learning set will need to understand the purposes and process clearly; their commitment to consistent participation is vital to the success of their set.

It is important also that line managers of learning set members understand the process and, where necessary, receive briefing on their role in providing support to the process. They will need to be available to discuss options and possibilities for action developed during learning set meetings and be supportive of the team leader in turning options into successful action.

MONITORING TEAM LEADER DEVELOPMENT

As the change manager you will need to keep track of individual development to ensure that team leaders have the required skills to support their teams. We recommend that you monitor and coordinate your organization's team leader development activities by doing the following:

- Ask team leaders to keep a 'learning log' as the basis for review discussions with the change manager and, in time, to provide support for future team leaders.
- Develop a list of team leader competencies (see the competencies suggested above). Ask individuals to self-rate themselves at regular intervals against each competency. This will both provide an overview of skill development and build a record of the coaching and support resources in specific competencies available within your organization.
- Identify individuals within the organization who are considered to be effective team leaders. Ask these individuals to support the learning set process and to mentor new team leaders. You may also consider meeting with identified mentors regularly to provide support and review progress.
- Note internal and external training events that prove effective in supporting individual learning needs. Ensure that recommended events are congruent with the TBW approach.

4.6   SELECTING TEAM MEMBERS

Individuals are usually recruited to work as part of a team because they have specific technical skills and experience that are necessary for the achievement of the team goal.

KNOWLEDGE, SKILLS AND ABILITIES FOR TEAMWORK

Assessing candidates against generic knowledge, skill and ability requirements (KSAs) has been found to be a relatively successful selection tool, and one which can enhance the effectiveness of teams.

Regardless of their task specialism or their preferred team role, there are certain attributes that all team members need to demonstrate if the team is to achieve its goal. Michael Stevens and Michael Campion (1994) have identified specific KSA requirements for effective teamwork, as summarized in Box 4.4.

BOX 4.4   KNOWLEDGE, SKILLS AND ABILITIES FOR TEAMWORKING

I Interpersonal Team Member KSAs

A Conflict resolution	1 Fostering useful conflict, while eliminating dysfunctional conflict
	2 Matching the conflict management strategy to the source and nature of the conflict
	3 Using integrative (win–win) strategies rather than distributive (win–lose) strategies
B Collaborative problem solving	4 Utilizing the right level of participation for any given problem
	5 Avoiding obstacles to team problem solving (e.g. domination by some team members) by structuring how team members interact
C Communication	6 Employing communication patterns that maximize an open flow
	7 Using an open and supportive style of communication
	8 Utilizing active listening techniques
	9 Paying attention to nonverbal messages
	10 Taking advantage of the interpersonal value found in greeting other team members, engaging in appropriate small talk, etc.

II Self-management team KSAs

D Goal setting and performance management	11 Setting specific, challenging and acceptable team goals
	12 Monitoring, evaluating and providing feedback on performance
E Planning and task coordination	13 Coordinating and synchronizing tasks, activities and information
	14 Establishing fair and balanced roles and workloads among team members

Source: Stevens and Campion (1994). Reprinted with permission

TEAM COMPOSITION

When discussing team composition we refer to the 'mix' of members making up a team or the diversity amongst members of the team. Traditionally, individuals seem to have been selected for teams because it was thought they would 'fit', that is, because they were similar in many ways to the existing team members. Indeed, in traditionally structured organizations team members would also probably have similar skills. This homogeneity of team membership seems to produce stability within the team and may contribute to long-term viability. However, such teams may become less effective over time, particularly in generating new ideas, and they may also become insular and fail to respond to changes in their environment.

Today's organization teams have to respond to increased complexity in the environment, and they bring together people from diverse technical backgrounds. Such diverse teams therefore embody different attitudes and working practices as a result of differences in age, gender, ethnicity, educational background, nationality, organization culture, and so on. These differences need to be taken into account when designing effective teams, during the selection of team members, and even more importantly during team training and development. Moreover, as indicated in the previous chapter, personality factors are important (see p.51).

Perhaps the easiest form of diversity within teams to manage is that of differences between individual skills. Research indicates that high levels of team performance are linked to the task-related ability of team members. In today's competitive environment, organizations are developing the notion of 'skill mix' to ensure the most effective use of scarce resources – particularly highly specialized and highly paid skills.

At the end of this third stage the organization will have completed the basic groundwork involved in implementing TBW. The bed has been prepared to plant the seeds of teamworking. Issues of structure and culture have been examined, the appropriate support systems have been erected, team leaders have been selected and trained, and team member competencies have been identified. Next, the teams are set up to perform their tasks. Most organizations implementing teamworking tend to skip these preparatory steps. Consequently, teams are planted in metaphorical beds that do not support their growth and they often fail or remain isolated pockets of good practice in an organizational wasteland. If these initial stages have been addressed, the ISG can now turn to the task of developing effective teams throughout the organization – the topic of Chapter 5.

REFERENCES AND FURTHER READING

Argyris, C. (1991). *Reasoning, Learning, and Action: Individual and Organizational*. San Francisco: Jossey-Bass.

Bass, B. (1990). *Bass & Stogdill's Handbook of Leadership: Theory, Research and Managerial Applications* (3rd edn.). New York: Free Press.

Beyerlein, M.M., Johnson, D.A., & Beyerlein, S.T. (eds.) (1996). *Advances in the Interdisciplinary Study of Work Teams, vol. 2: Knowledge Work in Teams*. London: JAI Press.

Eagly, A.H., & Johnson, B.T. (1990). Leader and leadership style: A meta-analysis. *Journal of Applied Psychology*, 108: 233–56.

Hackman, J.R. (2002). *Leading Teams: Setting the Stage for Great Performances*. Cambridge, MA: Harvard Business School Press.

Heron, J. (1989). *The Facilitator's Handbook*. London: Kogan Page.

McGill, I. & Beatty, L. (1992). *Action Learning: A Practitioner's Guide*. London: Kogan Page.

Schein, E.H. (1985). *Organizational Culture and Leadership*. San Francisco: Jossey-Bass.

Stevens, M.J. & Campion, M.A. (1994). The knowledge, skill, and ability requirements for teamwork: Implications for human resource management. *Journal of Management*, 20: 503–30.

Weinstein, K. (1995). *Action Learning: A Journey in Discovery and Development*. New York: HarperCollins.

West, M.A. & Allen, N. (1997). Selection for teamwork. In N.R. Anderson and P. Herriot (eds.), *International Handbook of Selection and Assessment*. Chichester, UK: Wiley, pp 493–506.

Yukl, G. (1998). *Leadership in Organizations* (4th edn.). London: Prentice Hall.

5

DEVELOPING EFFECTIVE TEAMS

KEY AIMS

- Deciding on tasks and objectives for teams,
- Developing effective teamwork.

KEY TASKS

- Determining a task that is appropriate for teamwork,
- Defining team vision, mission and objectives,
- Ensuring team participation,
- Developing high quality team decision making,
- Nurturing team creativity and innovation.

KEY PEOPLE

- Team leaders and team members,
- Implementation steering group (ISG),
- Top management team.

This chapter addresses the question of how to ensure teams work effectively. This includes determining the tasks that teams will perform, team vision, mission, and their specific objectives. The chapter also examines how teams can ensure effective levels of participation (interaction, information sharing and influence over decision making), high quality of team decision making, and nurture creativity and innovation. This stage in team development focuses on the processes involved as team members begin to work together. The chapter describes how the change manager and ISG can constructively support team members through the inevitable tensions of working in a new way as they develop. Part of achieving this requires an understanding that teams go through predictable developmental stages from the early formation stage through to the stage where the team's life comes to an end. We therefore begin by briefly outlining the stages of team development.

Several experts have suggested sequences to describe and understand the development of teams. Tuckman's model, one of the best-known and most widely used (Tuckman, 1965), suggests five stages: forming, storming, norming, performing and adjourning.

There is often considerable anxiety at the *forming* stage. Team members ask testing questions which reflect their concern about roles – particularly the nature of the leadership role – and about the resources available to the team. Individuals within the team seek out information about other team members, particularly their backgrounds and experience in the type of work that the team will undertake. They are likely to be anxious about external expectations of the team, and to request information about rules and regulations that will affect the team's working methods. At this early stage, team members may be rather guarded in the information they divulge. Their early judgements of one another will therefore be based on limited information. The most important task at this stage is to ensure that team goals are clearly stated and agreed.

During the *storming* stage, conflict emerges between individuals and subgroups. The choice, authority and/or competency of the leader are challenged, and individuals resist attempts by the leader to control team processes. The value and feasibility of the team task is questioned.

Hidden tensions surface during this stage. Individuals may react strongly and opinions may become polarized. This stage can also see an emerging honesty and openness within the team as they work through the conflicts. The team leader must build positively on this to gain shared commitment to the team goals, to build trust, begin the definition of team roles and to establish conflict resolution strategies for the team.

During *norming*, conflicts are resolved and the team begins to address the task with positive cooperation. Plans are made and work standards are established. Norms or agreed rules and ways of working emerge regarding team and individual behaviour. Team members more readily communicate their views and feelings, and networks for mutual support emerge. During this stage the team leader should allow the team to take more responsibility for its own planning and team processes, perhaps allowing team members to make mistakes and encouraging the team to reflect upon them. It is important to ensure that norms are established that meet the needs of the organization since teams could develop norms that are destructive to effective functioning (e.g. it's acceptable to be late or not to turn up for team meetings).

At the *performing* stage, team members begin to see successful outcomes as their energies focus constructively on the joint task. They settle into an effective teamworking structure, within which individual members feel comfortable, and begin to work together more flexibly. The team leader can usually withdraw from day-to-day involvement, a change that is acknowledged and accepted by team members. At this stage, systems of regular review should be established to ensure that the team continues to be effective and responsive to its environment.

Not all teams go through the final *adjourning* stage as a team, but at various times of its life key members will leave or major projects will be completed or curtailed. It is important that the effects of such changes on the life of the team should be acknowledged: teams may revert to earlier stages of development depending on their levels of maturity, their stability and the scale of the change.

Not all teams will fit neatly into Tuckman's sequence of team development. A team might go back and forth, revisiting stages to deal with them gradually at different levels. Change managers and team leaders can encourage effective, productive teams by introducing an effective team-development process and ensuring that the team task is clear, conflicts are processed with satisfactory (and ideally creative) consequences, team members' roles are clear, positive norms are established, the team performs well, and disbands constructively and in a timely fashion when its task is complete.

If you are the change manager you are responsible, in cooperation with the team leader, for selecting and implementing activities to improve team effectiveness, for increasing team viability, and for promoting team member growth and well-being at all stages of team development. What, though, are the major components required for effective teamwork? There are four key aspects that must be addressed – the team's task and vision; participation in the team (interaction, information sharing, influence over decision making); high quality decision making; and encouraging creativity and innovation. We consider each of these in turn.

5.1 TEAM TASKS, VISIONS AND OBJECTIVES

TEAM TASKS

For a team to be creative it must have a clear task appropriate for team performance and a vision to give focus and direction to creative energies. The ISG must decide what tasks teams will perform in the organization and can consider two questions:

1 What tasks currently exist that can best be performed by a team?
2 How can existing tasks be transformed to make them appropriate for teamwork?

Research within psychology and organizational behaviour suggests the following dimensions can be used to analyse the content of tasks in the organization:

- *Completeness*: i.e. whole tasks – not simply putting the studs on the car wheels but assembling the whole transmission system plus wheels.
- *Varied demands*: the task requires a range of skills that are held or best developed by a number of different individuals.
- *Requirements for interdependence and interaction*: the task requires people to work together in interdependent ways, communicating, sharing information, and debating decisions about the best way to do the job.
- *Task significance*: the importance of the task in contributing to organizational goals or to the wider society. A lifeboat team in a rural coastal area with busy shipping lanes and a health and safety team in a high-risk industry are likely to be highly intrinsically motivated by the significance of their tasks.
- *Opportunities for learning*: providing team members with chances to develop and stretch their skills and knowledge.

- *Development possibilities for the task*: the task can be developed to offer more challenges to the team members, requiring them to take on more responsibility and learn new skills over time. The shopfloor manufacturing team might develop responsibility for direct interaction with customers over lead time from ordering to delivery of products as well as pricing of products.
- *Autonomy*: this refers to the amount of freedom teams have over how to do their work, from something as mundane as when to take breaks, through to making decisions about new products or new staff. Organizations consistently fail to delegate sufficient responsibility to teams, and middle managers jealously guard their power by limiting team autonomy. The degree of autonomy of the team can be assessed in relation to team influence over:
  - The formulation of goals – what and how much it is expected to produce,
  - Where to work and number of hours (when to work overtime and when to leave),
  - Choice about further activities beyond the given task,
  - Selection of production methods,
  - Internal distribution of task responsibilities within the group,
  - Membership of the group (who and how many people will work in the group),
  - Leadership – whether there will be a leader and who will be the leader,
  - How to carry out individual tasks.

The ISG can evaluate existing tasks by asking those likely to be team members to rate tasks on each of the six dimensions of appropriateness for team working above on a five-point scale (ranging from 1 'very little' to 5 'a great deal'). A lifeboat team charged with responsibility for saving people in stricken vessels is likely to rate each of the dimensions (completeness, varied demands, requirements for interdependence, task significance, opportunities for learning, task development, and autonomy) very highly. A group of people responsible for typing the correct postcodes onto wrongly addressed envelopes in the postal service is likely to rate them all very low. This analysis therefore enables the ISG to answer the first question: 'What tasks currently exist that can best be performed by a team?' To answer the second – 'How can existing tasks be transformed to make them appropriate for teamwork?' – they can apply the same analysis to redesign the work.

TEAM VISIONS

Having decided on the team tasks, the next stage is to determine a vision or inspirational direction for the team. Vision is not some empty mission statement espousing motherhood and apple pie and hiding a poverty of orientation in action. Vision for a team should be a clear, shared, negotiated, attainable, and evolving ideal of some valued future outcome. To a primary health care team it might be enabling patients to take responsibility for their health by giving them a sense of power and control over their own physical health outcomes. For an R&D team it could be developing a new form of a pharmaceutical product that minimizes side effects for cancer patients receiving chemotherapy. There are a number of dimensions along which the vision of a team can be understood.

Vision clarity

In order for a team to determine its objectives, goals and actions it must have a clear vision. If team members are unsure of what the shared orientations, values and purposes of their colleagues are, it is difficult for them to articulate a clear statement which encapsulates these orientations and values. This requires that team members communicate about their work values and orientations. They must then find a form of words which expresses accurately and clearly these shared values, interests and motivations.

Shared vision

One feature of teams which are successful against low odds is that they have a clear shared vision – a vision of what the team wants to accomplish in the future which represents the values and beliefs of the individuals within the team. *Vision is a shared idea of a valued outcome which provides the motivation for the team's work.*

If team members do not share a team vision, their individual creativity cannot be pooled to produce creative team outcomes. This implies that visions are also negotiated, because members of teams do not come together with identical values and visions. When the team leader or organizational hierarchy determine, rather than influence, the 'vision' for a team, the vision is unlikely to be shared and will have little influence upon creativity. Where there is a strong shared sense of valued goals or orientations within a team, it is much more likely that commitment and creativity will be engendered and employed. Visions must therefore be negotiated by team members coming together, working through their differences to find a consensual sense of their valued orientation.

Evolving visions

The foregoing necessarily implies that a vision should be evolving. Visions are reflections of human values, interests, expectancies, and beliefs. Because people develop and change and because teams develop and change, the vision itself must evolve over time. A vision that is not reviewed and modified as part of team development becomes merely a marker of their past.

Dimensions of team vision

To gain maximum advantage, team visions need to incorporate the following features:

1 *Clarity*: In order for the team to determine its objectives, goals and action plans, it needs a clearly articulated vision. Time must be set aside for team members to communicate about their work values, interests and motivations and to develop a clear and agreed statement of that vision.

2 *Motivating value*: The values that we bring to our work influence the amount of effort that we put into it. Where the team vision closely reflects the underlying values of the team it is likely to promote motivation, team loyalty, effort and commitment. It may be that the content of the work which the organization currently requires of the team (e.g. requiring a focus by an R&D team only on short-term shareholder value rather than long-term research discoveries) cannot easily be matched to individual values. This can lead to dissatisfaction and poor performance over time.

3 *Attainability*: There can be a tendency for teams to get carried away during 'visioning' workshops – developing vision

statements which at first sight are wildly exciting but on reflection will demotivate because of their magnitude or difficulty. There is a fine balance to be maintained between visions that excite and motivate team members and ones that are dismissed because individuals do not believe that they are attainable.

4   *Sharedness*: The degree to which visions are shared by all team members is an important factor in predicting the effectiveness of the team. The achievement of a shared vision comes from the involvement of all team members in its negotiation. By definition a team vision cannot be imposed from outside.

5   *Ability to develop*: The team vision should never be regarded as cast in stone. Teams, individuals, organizations and society are constantly evolving, and it is important that the team vision evolves in the same way. The vision should be regularly reviewed in order to ensure that it is alive, up-to-date and representative of the changing values and orientations of team members, thus enabling the team to develop in new and appropriate directions.

Elements of team vision

There are eight major elements upon which a team's vision may focus:

1   *Consistency with organizational objectives.*   In some circumstances a team may decide that it is important for its own values, purposes and orientations to act as a minority group which aims to bring about change in organizational objectives. For example, within the UK National Health Service there has been considerable debate about the conflict which exists between providing health care and reducing spending. Some teams have attempted to subvert the second orientation where they see it as conflicting with their aim of providing quality health care for all, regardless of priorities determined by a Regional Health Authority. So, in some circumstances, a team may work effectively when its vision contradicts stated organizational objectives. However, it is very important that teams are clear about when they wish to act as minority groups in order that they may develop appropriate strategies to bring about the kinds of organizational change they wish.

2   *Customer/service receiver needs.*   To what extent will the team work to meet the needs of its customers, whether they be

customers within or outside the organization? To what extent are service receivers seen as people who are to be merely satisfied or placated, rather than people who are to receive the best quality of service available? For example, a teaching team in a university department might prefer to emphasize research excellence above the quality of teaching provided to students. Alternatively, they may strive to admit as many students as possible, putting pedagogical excellence second. A car maintenance team may emphasize satisfying the customer above ever-increasing profitability (though these two may not necessarily contradict one another).

3 *Quality of product, service or function.* A major emphasis within organizations at the beginning of the twenty-first century is the quality of services and functioning within organizational settings. Team members may also discuss the extent to which top quality will characterize their own working relationships. This may be reflected in the speed with which requests for information within the team are met, and also the quality of information which is eventually produced.

4 *Value to wider society.* It is unusual for teams to take time out to consider the value of their work for the wider society. Consideration of this and ways in which it can be enhanced is an important way of encouraging both team cohesion and greater team effectiveness. Such consideration may promote conflict if team members perceive their work to be irrelevant to the wider society or if there are conflicts between team members about the potential value of the team's work. However, such conflict enables team members to achieve clear perception of the purposes of their work and therefore enhances team effectiveness and creativity.

5 *Team climate relationships.* Team climate relationships are often neglected when teams discuss their functioning. If team members have such difficult relationships that members are inclined to leave the team, long-term team viability is threatened. Teams therefore need to consider the type of team climate they wish to create. Team climate refers to aspects of teamwork such as warmth, humour, amount of conflict, mutual support, sharing, backbiting, emphasis of status, participation, information sharing, level of criticism of each other's work, and support for new ideas.

6 *Growth and well-being of team members.* Another element of vision is support for the skill development and well-being of team members. Growth, skill development and challenge are

central elements of work life and teams can be a major source of support. They may provide opportunities for skill sharing and support for new training. One issue is the extent to which team members will support skill development and training which may further someone's career, although this may not contribute immediately to team effectiveness. Another area of concern for a team is the general well-being of its members. This is especially true for those working in conditions of high stress, such as caring professionals. The social support which team members provide can have a buffering effect, preventing stress-related illnesses.

7   *Relationships with other teams and departments in the organ-ization.*   Teams rarely operate in isolation. They interact with other teams and departments within the organization, for example in cooperating in cross-functional teams or competing for scarce resources. Therefore teams need to decide what orientation – co-operation or competition – they will adopt towards other teams and departments within their organization. In almost all cases cooperation will benefit, and competition between teams will hinder, organizational effectiveness.

8   *Relationships outside the organization.*   In order for a team to have a clear shared vision about its work, it must make explicit (where relevant) the quality and nature of relationships it seeks with parent organizations, and those outside the organization (e.g. other organizations).

Not all of these elements of team vision will be relevant to all teams in equal measure. However, team members will benefit from full discussion of each element in order to achieve the completeness of vision that is required for long-term, effective teamworking. Allowing team members to work together to define and agree a shared vision is important at this stage. Team members may find the task of generating a vision statement from scratch rather daunting but the activity of thinking through each of these elements will help team members to think deeply about both the team's purpose and about the way in which they want the team to operate.

From the team vision it is a small but important step to setting objectives. Team leaders or change managers can facilitate team goals that are specific and challenging (rather than vaguely speci-fied and easily attained); agree mechanisms for regular feedback on goal attainment in order to maintain performance levels; explore the resource and training needs of team members to ensure they can achieve their objectives; formally and publicly reward the achievement of objectives in appropriate relation to the importance of their achievement to the team as a whole; provide support if required in prioritizing goals, developing action plans and managing time.

A well-used approach to setting objectives for both individual team members and the team as a whole is the use of SMART dimensions:

- Specific
- Measurable
- Appropriate
- Realistic
- Time-bound.

Even more instructive is what the research evidence from psychological studies of goal setting and motivation indicate. Goals should be *clear*, they should also be *challenging* and team members responsible for achieving them should be *involved* in setting them. Finally, team members should feel a sense of *efficacy* about their ability as a team to achieve these goals. In these circumstances, goals are likely to be maximally motivating and the team maximally effective.

5.2   TEAM PARTICIPATION

The point of teamwork is to bring together people with different skills, experiences and knowledge to work interdependently to accomplish a task that is best done by such a group rather than by individuals working alone or in parallel. So building effective teams means ensuring a high and appropriate level of participation. This requires that they interact, share information and also influence the decisions that are made. We next examine what this means and how it can be enabled.

INTERACTION

In order for a group of individuals who share a common goal to be called a team they must have some minimal ongoing interaction, otherwise their efforts are essentially uncoordinated and unaggregated. Teams interact during task performance and informally; both are equally important. Informal interactions might include parties, lunches or informal chats in the corridors to discuss family matters or sporting events. These interactions strengthen the social bonding, cohesion and familiarity which enable people to feel safe with one another. Interaction during task performance provides an exchange of information, communication, and so on, which enables the team to coordinate individual member efforts to achieve their shared goals. Without regular meetings, both formal and informal, important information is not exchanged and assumptions and expectations may be built up which are not matched by reality. Indeed our research results reveal that even poor team meetings are better than no team meetings at all, since members get to exchange information in small informal dyads or groups before, after and even during meetings. Without sufficient interaction, team members may begin to diverge in their views about what is important for the team, and perceptions of other team members' actions may be incorrect. Misapprehension and misunderstanding can lead to conflict and lack of coordination in terms of task processes. These in turn lead to lowered team effectiveness.

It is not possible to specify any ideal frequency of interaction. Some teams will need to meet more often than others, and meetings between some team members will need to be more frequent than between other team members. However, teams should meet *minimally* once a month, in order to update one another on developments. It is also valuable for teams to take time out every six months to reflect upon and modify as necessary their objectives, their strategies for achieving those objectives and team processes such as communication and the participation in decision making (a topic we return to in the next chapter).

INFORMATION SHARING

Information in a team context is data which alters the understanding of the team as a whole and/or of individual team members. Monitoring information is essential for team effectiveness. Information can be rich or poor to the extent that it alters understanding; that is, the more it alters understanding the richer it is. For example, in a changeover of teams in a chemical processing plant, information relating to potentially volatile reactions noted during the previous shift is rich information. It communicates the likelihood of risk to the team taking over. On the other hand, a computer printout of the number of visits to children under five years of age made by a health visitor during the course of one month may communicate relatively little information to her supervisor, since it provides no indication of the difficulty of the visits or the quality of the work.

The medium of transfer of information is determined by its richness. The least rich information is transferred by paper or e-mail messages. Slightly richer information is given in the form of telephone conversations or video conferencing, but information is most richly transferred when people talk face to face. Voice inflexion, facial expression, body posture and gestures all add to the richness of information transfer. Moreover, in face-to-face meetings it is possible to ask questions and explore issues in depth.

Within a team setting the ideal medium is face to face except for routine messages. However, there is a temptation to avoid such direct communication since this may take up time. The whole basis of team work is communication, coordination, cooperation and transfer of information in the richest possible form. Consequently there is a real need for team members to address issues about information sharing and communication and to examine the media that they plan to use to transfer this information.

Increasingly, individuals find themselves working within dispersed teams, often with colleagues who live in different countries or in other situations which provide little opportunity for informal or regular communication. Such teams need formal, regular communication and meetings where there are opportunities to chat informally or socialize to help increase cohesion and trust. An international computer company which has outlawed 'personal chat' via e-mail may have saved a minimal amount on telephone charges, but they have lost a great deal more through the reinforcement of already pervasive divisions within their international teams.

INFLUENCE OVER DECISION MAKING

Traditionally, the notion of participation has been understood as the extent of influence over decision making and it is to this topic that we now turn. Participation can involve simply superficial consultation where team members' views are sought but in practice the team leader or team managers make decisions based on their own judgement. At the other extreme is total democracy where all decisions are taken by a team vote; but this can lead to decision-making 'paralysis' rather than team effectiveness.

There are many situations where teams need leaders. In moments of crisis there may not be time for the whole team to discuss the appropriate course of action in depth. One individual may be required to grasp the nettle and take decisions for the good of the whole team. In most circumstances, however, teams can sanction individuals to take the decision in specific areas of the team's activity. In order to achieve a balance between excessive democracy and authoritarianism, team reviews of decision-making processes should be conducted every six months to a year. The purpose of these reviews should be to determine which team members should take executive decisions on behalf of the team and in which areas.

Part of enabling participation in the team is ensuring that each team member is clear about his or her role in the drama of the team's production. Lack of clarity about team roles can lead to feelings of distrust, lack of respect and conflict among team members, obvious work overload or underload for some individuals (likely to be interpreted as shirking), or confusion about the team leader's role. Role negotiation exercises help to clarify roles and how they contribute to the achievement of team objectives:

1 Team members list on a piece of flipchart paper their individual objectives and agreed actions and indicate how these relate to the team's overall objectives.
2 They clarify one another's objectives in discussion.
3 Team members then post requests on one another's lists for less, more or the same level of particular behaviours and for new behaviours.
4 Working in pairs, they consider the comments on their sheets and negotiate an agreed view about action points arising from the various requests.
5 Participants hang their flipchart sheets on the wall. The team as a whole asks questions about each of the sheets and offers suggestions.

Through such role negotiation exercises, the roles of individuals can be more effectively defined and they can function more productively in achieving their objectives and those of the team as a whole. Role negotiation can improve team effectiveness considerably, overcoming many of the problems of process loss and team coordination associated with teamworking. By building trust between team members, and providing them with an opportunity to use mutual influence and negotiation, it also promotes change in team behaviours and improvement in team functioning.

5.3   QUALITY OF DECISION MAKING

A principle assumption behind the structuring of organizational functioning into work groups is that groups will make better decisions than individual group members working alone. However, a good deal of research has shown that groups are subject to social processes which undermine their decision-making effectiveness. While work groups tend to make decisions which are better than the average of decisions made by individual members, they consistently fall short of the quality of decisions made by the best individual member. The implications of this for the functioning of boards and senior executive teams are considerable. Organizational behaviourists and social psychologists have therefore devoted considerable effort to identifying the social processes which create deficiencies in group decision making:

1   *Personality factors* can affect social behaviour in various ways. For example, any shyness by individual members, who may be hesitant to offer their opinions and knowledge assertively, will mean that they fail to contribute fully to the group's store of knowledge.

2   Group members are subject to *social conformity* effects causing them to withhold opinions and information contrary to the majority view – especially an organizationally dominant view.

3   Group members may lack *communication skills* and so be unable to present their views and knowledge successfully. The person who has mastered impression management within the organization may disproportionately influence group decisions even in the absence of expertise.

4   The group may be *dominated* by particular individuals who take up disproportionate 'air time' or argue so vigorously with the opinion of others that their own views prevail. It is noteworthy that 'air time' and expertise are correlated in high-performing groups and uncorrelated in groups that perform poorly.

5   Particular group members may be *egocentric* (such as senior organizational members whose egocentricity may have carried them to the top) and consequently unwilling to

consider opinions or knowledge offered by other group members contrary to their own.

6   *Status and hierarchy* effects can cause some members' contributions to be valued and attended to disproportionately. When a senior executive is present in a meeting, his or her views are likely to have an undue influence on the outcome.

7   *'Risky shift'* refers to the tendency of work groups to make more extreme decisions than the average of individual members' opinions or decision. Group decisions tend to be either more risky or more conservative than the average of individual members' opinions or decisions. Thus shifts in the extremeness of decisions affecting the competitive strategy of an organization can occur simply as a result of group processes rather than for rational or well-judged reasons.

8   In his study of failures in policy decisions, social psychologist Irving Janis identified the phenomenon of 'groupthink' (Janis, 1982), whereby tightly knit groups may err in their decision making because they are more concerned with achieving agreement than with the quality of the decisions made. This can be especially threatening to organizational functioning where different departments see themselves as competing with one another, promoting 'in-group' favouritism and groupthink.

9   The *social loafing effect* is the tendency of individuals in group situations to work less hard than they do when individual contributions can be identified and evaluated. In organizations, individuals may put less effort into achieving quality decisions in meetings, if they perceive that their contribution is hidden in overall group performance.

10 *Diffusion of responsibility* can inhibit individuals from taking responsibility for action when in the presence of others. People seem to assume that responsibility will be shouldered by others who are present in a situation requiring action. In organizational settings, individuals may fail to act in a crisis involving the functioning of expensive technology, assuming that others in their team are taking the responsibility for making the necessary decisions. Consequently, the overall quality of group decisions is threatened.

11 The study of brainstorming groups shows that quantity and often quality of ideas produced by individuals working separately are consistently superior to those produced by a group working together. This is due to a *'production-blocking'* effect. Individuals are inhibited from both thinking of new

ideas and offering them aloud to the group by the competing verbalizations of others.

One approach to overcoming these problems when a significant issue has to be addressed is to use a 'stepladder' approach to decision making. Each group member is given time to think through the particular problem or issue before sending a document to the group presenting his or her views. Each member sends his or her preliminary views about the appropriate course of action before viewing others' preliminary solutions. A final decision is delayed until all members of the group have had an opportunity to present their views and there has been a full and inclusive face-to-face discussion. This approach gives each member of the team time to reflect upon the particular problem in order to prepare his or her case, independent of other group members. It also gives time for some discussion to take place about all the presentations. Decision making is thus postponed until all group members have presented their views.

This approach to decision making facilitates communication since all members of the group have an opportunity to present their views. Such communication may lead to a greater number or range of ideas being presented, since conformity processes will be minimized. It also inhibits social loafing effects since individual accountability is emphasized and there is no opportunity for individual members to hide behind others' contributions. Furthermore, because each member is required to present his or her views without the benefit of having heard all the other team members' views, disagreements are more likely and therefore the quality of decision making and discussion may be improved. The group is exposed to the continual input of fresh ideas which have not been affected by group norms, and this may lead to a vigorous evaluation and exploration of contrasting ideas. Such exploration of divergent opinions within teams leads to better quality decision making. Moreover, research evidence indicates that there is no difference in the time taken for decision making between groups using the stepladder technique and conventional techniques. However, the quality of group decision scores is generally significantly better than in conventional groups.

High quality decision making is also characterized by *constructive controversy*. In well-functioning teams, there is a high level of 'constructive controversy' where team members feel their competence is affirmed rather than attacked, where there is a climate of cooperation and trust rather than a climate of competition and distrust, and where critical review is seen as a constructive process rather than a destructive, aggressive conflict. In such teams there is a concern more with excellence of outcomes and less with the individualistic ambitions of team members.

The extent to which a team can tolerate within its membership a minority who adopt differing views is an important determinant of good decision making. Much, if not all, creativity and innovation is applied in practice via conflict – that is, by overcoming resistance to change in others. The team itself may be a minority within an organization, not just encouraging new and improved ways of doing things, but, by its stands, encouraging independent and creative thinking and acting more widely within the organization. Minorities influence others through processes of conversion and conflict, which enable other minorities to express their differing creative views. All of which is of great importance in organizations that seek to adapt to the ever-changing and increasingly complex world we are creating. How a team manages a minority within its membership is an important indicator of its ability to be a creative adaptive social unit.

5.4   SUPPORT FOR INNOVATION

Teams are seedbeds of creativity and innovation because they bring together people with different knowledge, skills, experiences and attitudes. The engagement of this diversity to a common task is always likely (in well-functioning teams) to produce rich sources of creativity and innovation. Support for innovation has two distinct elements: espoused support and active support. In many teams support for innovation is espoused, but when the practicalities of support are examined, it is rare for team members or top management to give time, resources and cooperation for the development of new ideas. Yet it is precisely these activities that determine the extent to which creativity within teams occurs. If new ideas are accepted and encouraged verbally but team members do not provide the necessary practical support, the platitudes of verbal encouragement soon lose their currency.

Creative thinking techniques can also be used but they are not magic solutions. Creativity is 95 per cent hard work and 5 per cent lucky discovery. However brilliant innovative ideas may be, putting them into practice demands considerable commitment and effort. It requires courage to use creativity techniques within teams that are not used to working in this way. Creativity and innovation always involve risk. But if the team is persistent in introducing new ways of working, such techniques will bring success and so develop confidence and skill within the team. Below are brief outlines of some of these techniques that teams can be taught to use, and fuller detailed guidelines are offered in the accompanying CD.

1   *Classical brainstorming*. In classic brainstorming, team members produce and note as many ideas as possible, however fantastic they may seem. Participants should suspend judgement and accept all ideas offered. It is entirely appropriate to 'piggy-back' – to use others' ideas to stimulate other, new ideas. The best way to conduct a brainstorming session is to give individuals an opportunity to generate ideas on their own first, to write them down and bring them to the group situation. This avoids the problem of groups becoming stuck in a narrow line of thought about a problem. It also allows the group discussion to piggyback on individuals' ideas and generates a sense of fun. This creative group environment can produce wilder ideas which may well contain the seed of a very different and new approach to the task or issue which the team is facing.

2   *Brainwriting pool*.   This technique has the advantage of generating large numbers of relevant ideas in a short space of time. Team members, seated around a table, note five to ten ideas on blank sheets of paper (e.g. on the different potential uses of empty cereal boxes), then place them in the middle of the table. Each member then adds more ideas on the sheets already started by each of the other members. One advantage of this technique is that, if team members find it difficult to convene a meeting, sheets can be circulated over a number of days and the results collated by a coordinator. Computer networks have enabled this system to become widespread in a form known as 'brain-netting': a file is set up containing the problem to be addressed and all members of the team contribute their ideas to the central file.

3   *Negative brainstorming*.   Negative brainstorming is useful when a potential course of action has been agreed by team members. The task is then to generate as many potential problems with the agreed solution within a fixed amount of time – perhaps 10 minutes. The team then reviews the ideas to identify ways of improving on the proposed solution. An example here might be to consider all of the potential or actual problems with air travel and then to think of ways of overcoming these problems.

4 *Goal orientation.* Goal orientation is a way of restating problems or objectives in order to find more creative perspectives from which to view them. This in turn can lead to creative solutions or objectives. For example, traffic jam problems could be restated as a series of problems: how to reduce the number of cars; how to increase the number of people in each vehicle; or – more wildly – how to 'teleport' people to their destinations instantly.

5 *Table of elements.* This is a technique for breaking a problem or issue down into a set of elements, brainstorming within each and then choosing from among the various components those ideas which may form the basis of a creative solution to the problem. Organizing a team party could, for instance, be broken down into *who* will be invited, *when* the party will be held, *what* refreshments and activities must be prepared, *why* the party should be held (celebration, reward, PR), *how* it will be organized, and so on.

6 *Stakeholder analysis.* This approach involves thinking through change proposals or team objectives from the perspective of those principally affected by the team's work. It can generate new ideas and, most importantly, fresh insights into how to approach and plan innovations in the team's work.

7 *Developing constructive debates.* Team members carefully describe their positions, explaining how they have come to their decisions in relation to any particular issue within the team. They also indicate to what extent they are confident or uncertain about the positions they have adopted. Those in the team with opposing viewpoints seek more information about others' positions and attempt to restate them as clearly as possible. There should be attempts to explore areas of common ground in opposing positions, along with an emphasis on personal regard for individuals whose positions oppose their own. This process leads to greater creativity and more productive outcomes. Team members finally encourage integration by working to resolve controversy, based on the principle of excellence in decision making. Attempts to influence team members towards a solution are based on shared, rational understanding rather than attempted dominance. Finally, team members strive for consensus by combining team ideas wherever possible rather than using techniques to reduce controversy, such as majority voting.

Creativity in organizations is associated with uncertainty, ambiguity, conflict and risk. The ideas offered here are not some easy remedy for teamwork without danger or difficulty. Developing a negotiated, shared and evolving vision means accepting uncertainty over time and encouraging, not minimizing, change. It also involves giving up some control to enable team members to develop their own vision, which may well be at variance with that of other teams in the organization. This is the stuff of creativity. There are risks and opportunities in participation, with team members taking, rather than avoiding, responsibility for decision making and maximizing rich means of communication. Such participation enables the group to become a vital, evolving social unit, the creative energies of which are released, but with unpredictable outcomes. Reflexivity involves challenge to existing ways of doing things. This may mean encouraging uncertainty in the face of rapid change, rather than attempting to minimize it, which is often our natural reaction. But our world is changing by our own making and old ways of responding to changing circumstances are no longer helpful. The creative response to change is to work with, rather than against, the forces of change.

5.5   TEAM CONFLICT RESOLUTION

There are times when team functioning is hindered by interpersonal conflict. Building effective teams also involves understanding why such conflict occurs and how it can best be dealt with. In productive and creative teams, debate is not only endemic but also desirable. Team diversity and differences should be a source of excellence, quality and creativity. But conflict experienced as threatening and unpleasant by team members can destroy relationships and lower the effectiveness of the team. This is especially likely when the conflict becomes personal, where team members attack one another or denigrate each other's skills, abilities or performance in some way. This is unhealthy both for the individuals concerned and for the team as a whole.

Work role or organization factors cause the largest proportion of interpersonal conflicts in teams, for example:

- lack of clarity or mutual understanding of roles,
- lack of structure in the team or the team task,
- the absence of clear, shared vision and explicit goals,
- inadequacy of resources,
- poor organization climate or inappropriate organization strategy,

- differences in functional orientation (e.g. sales versus production),
- status inconsistencies (e.g. finance assistant dealing with a senior manager's expenses claims),
- overlapping authority (it's not clear who is in charge),
- task interdependence (where team members have to rely on one another to complete their part of the task successfully),
- incompatible evaluation systems (e.g. quality of product versus speed of delivery versus cost of product).

Team leaders can identify and deal with such organizational factors where they are a cause of conflict by using good listening skills and a creative approach to conflict resolution, within which the aim is to creatively meet the underlying needs of both parties to the conflict.. Where it is not possible to remove a source of conflict, for example where extra resources for a project cannot be found, it is essential that all team members understand the true source of the problem and are involved in discussions about ways in which the team can work positively to overcome the resulting difficulties.

It is clearly best if individual team members can resolve differences with colleagues on a one-to-one basis in an open and constructive way when difficulties first arise. This will be easier in a climate of perceived safety within the team where the development of subgroups is positively discouraged. Team leaders can support their teams in the development of such a climate during its early stages by being optimistic, confident, encouraging and available. Indeed, conflict is least likely when team leaders continue to:

- create alignment around shared objectives and strategies to attain them;
- increase enthusiasm and excitement about the work and maintain a sense of optimism and confidence about success;
- help team members to appreciate each other;
- help them to learn how to confront and resolve differences constructively;
- help team members to coordinate activities, continuously improve, develop capabilities, encourage flexibility, objectively analyse processes, and learn collectively about better ways to work together;
- represent the interests of the team, protect its reputation, help to establish trust with external stakeholders and help to resolve conflicts between internal and external partners;
- create a unique team identity.

When individuals are unable to resolve their differences you may find it necessary to involve a third party to act as mediator. This might be the team leader or a team member who is respected by both parties. Some organization personnel departments train their members in how to resolve team conflicts. Teams can also call upon the services of a chartered occupational psychologist (lists of such psychologists working in the UK are available from the British Psychological Society) or a consultant trained in conflict resolution techniques.

This stage of developing team-based working (TBW) has focused on the importance of ensuring that teams have clear tasks, and tasks that are most appropriately undertaken by a team rather than by individuals. It is also the stage at which the team needs to be clear about its vision, based on the values of the organization and the individuals within the team. Sculpting an appropriate task and vision then naturally leads into clear objectives and action plans.

The next component of this stage is ensuring that the team works as a team, with appropriate levels of interaction, communication, information dissemination and shared influence over decisions. Moreover, effectively functioning teams will inevitably be sources of creative ideas and will implement innovation in the form of new products, services or ways of working. We might be tempted to think that the job of developing the team-based organization is done but it is vital that effective teamworking is sustained and that team performance is evaluated and feedback made available to the team. Sustaining and reviewing team performance are essential if teams are to maintain a high level of performance and to continuously improve. Stage 5 of developing TBW, the topic of the next chapter, describes how to implement robust processes for sustaining and reviewing performance.

REFERENCES AND FURTHER READING

Brown, R. (2000). *Group Processes* (2nd edn.). Oxford: Blackwell.

Campion, M.A., Medsker, G.J., & Higgs, A.C. (1993). Relations between work group characteristics and effectiveness: Implications for designing effective work groups. *Personnel Psychology*, 46: 823–50.

Cohen, S., Evans, G.W., Stokols, D., & Krantz, D.S. (1986). *Behaviour, Health and Environmental Stress*. New York: Plenum.

Cohen, S.G., & Bailey, D.E. (1997). What makes teams work: Group effectiveness research from the shop floor to the executive suite. *Journal of Management*, 23, 3: 239–90.

De Dreu, C.K.W., Harinck, F., & Van Vianen, A.E.M. (1999). Conflict and performance in groups and organizations. In C.L. Cooper & I.T. Robertson (eds.), *International Review of Industrial and Organizational Psychology* (vol. 14). Chichester, UK: Wiley, pp. 369–414.

Diehl, M., & Stroebe, W. (1987). Productivity loss in brainstorming groups: Towards the solution of a riddle. *Journal of Personality and Social Psychology*, 53: 497–509.

Edmondson, A.C. (1999). Psychological safety and learning behavior in work teams. *Administrative Science Quarterly*, 44: 350–83.

Flood, P., MacCurtain, S., & West, M.A. (2001). *Effective Top Management Teams*. Dublin, Ireland: Blackhall Press.

Gersick, C.J.G. (1989). Marking time: Predictable transitions in work groups. *Academy of Management Journal*, 32: 274–309.

Goodman, P.S. (1986). *Designing Effective Work Groups*. San Francisco: Jossey Bass.

Hackman, J.R. (1990). *Groups That Work (and Those That Don't)*. San Francisco: Jossey-Bass.

Janis, I.L. (1982). *Groupthink* (2nd edn.). Boston, MA: Houghton Mifflin.

Tuckman, B.W. (1965). Developmental sequences in small groups. *Psychological Bulletin*, 63: 348–99.

West, M.A., (1994). *Effective Teamwork*. Oxford: Blackwell.

West, M.A. (ed.) (1996). *Handbook of Work Group Psychology*. Chichester, UK: Wiley.

West, M., Borrill, C. and Unsworth, K. (1998). Team effectiveness in organizations. In C. Cooper and I. Robertson (eds.), *International Review of Industrial and Organizational Psychology* (vol. 13). Chichester, UK: Wiley, pp.1–48.

6

REVIEWING AND SUSTAINING TEAM EFFECTIVENESS

KEY AIMS

- Reviewing the performance of teams,
- Developing durable systems to sustain and improve performance.

KEY TASKS

- Developing appropriate measures of performance,
- Evaluating performance on key dimensions,
- Reflecting on performance,
- Planning to make changes,
- Implementing changes.

KEY PEOPLE

- Implementation steering group (ISG),
- Team leaders,
- Team members.

Teamworking is not easy. When we work alone there is usually no one to disagree with us and no one who has to be informed about our thinking or decisions. There is no need for negotiation and discussion, and no possibility of misunderstanding. We therefore have to work hard in teams, though people generally find that this way of working is more enjoyable and less stressful than working alone. Consequently, it is important to evaluate the team's performance and to find ways of sustaining good performance and of improving performance in areas where this is warranted.

If team-based working (TBW) is to achieve the potential organization benefits, it must develop throughout the organization over time. A sustained commitment to monitoring team effectiveness and providing feedback to teams on their performance is therefore essential both to the development of individual teams and to the expansion of TBW within the organization as a whole. Effective feedback processes will enable existing teams to improve their own performance, while giving publicity to team successes, and this will create the energy and incentive for new teams to be created.

Your key responsibilities are to:

- ensure processes are in place for the identification of performance indicators at organization and team levels,
- develop a set of appropriate measurement tools,
- coordinate the assessment of individual teams,
- monitor feedback processes,
- make proposals for changes to team design at an organization level.

6.1   STEPS IN DESIGNING AN EFFECTIVE EVALUATION SYSTEM

We recommend nine steps involved in designing and implementing an effective evaluation system:

1   *Identify the team responsible for the evaluation process.*   This team (ideally the ISG) should have enough authority to ensure evaluation processes are carried out. If this is not the ISG it should report to the ISG.

2   *Identify performance indicators and measurement tools.*   The performance indicators you use should assess the influence of TBW practices in your organization. Because teams provide a complex environment for assessment, it is useful to augment

questionnaire-based surveys with other means of eliciting information about the way in which teams are working, such as focus groups and interviews. We provide (in 6.2) examples of self-report questionnaires that cover the main areas of team performance and which best predict success in teamworking. *Wherever possible it is important to gather information about team performance from customers or those who receive services from teams.* Also, as we indicated in Stage 1, getting evaluations of the cooperativeness of the team from other teams and departments provides important information about the team from sources external to them.

3   *Design the evaluation process.*   Plan for such activities as:

- *Communicating the purposes of the evaluation process*: it is important to let people within the organization know in advance that the evaluation is to take place. Also let them know that the purpose is to assess how effectively TBW is established within the organization and what additional supports need to be put in place. Reassure them that the purpose is not to evaluate individuals but to evaluate the processes of TBW.
- *Training those involved in data collection*: take the time to train people to administer questionnaires or conduct interviews. It is particularly important to ensure that, where appropriate, confidentiality of people's responses is respected. It is also important to try to ensure that the way data are collected across different teams is standardized so that variation in responses can be interpreted correctly. For example, if in one team the leader gathers information about leadership in the team, whereas in another an independent third party gathers information, variation between the teams in responses could be due to the difference in interviewers or questionnaire administrators.
- *Decide how to gather data*: it may be that all of the questionnaires will be used with each team in the organization. Also each team member may be interviewed, using the sample interview questions described below (see p.141). Alternatively, some teams may have interviews while all teams are administered questionnaire surveys.
- *Analysis of data*: it is relatively straightforward to analyse the data from the questionnaires included in this book by following the instructions given. Interpreting data from interviews is a little less straightforward and it is important that both interviewers and data analyses are guided by the responses of those interviewed. The interviewers should try to avoid their own prejudices influencing their interpretation of the data.

- *Feedback to team members and organizational representatives*: when people take the time to complete questionnaires or respond to interviewers' questions they are understandably interested to find out what the data reveal. It is therefore good practice to feed back the results of questionnaire surveys and interviews to those who have participated in the process.
- *Repeat evaluation*: one of the major strengths of instituting an evaluation process, particularly one which relies partly on questionnaires, is that the process can be repeated regularly (e.g. every year) and then it becomes possible to monitor TBW to identify change over time. It is enormously beneficial to repeat the evaluation process on a regular basis, especially if large parts of the evaluation process remain the same.

4   *Identify the respondents.*   Once teams have been established you will need to decide how many people to include in the evaluation survey: everyone within every team, everyone within selected teams, a sample from every team, and so on? How many customers or service receivers will be contacted and what questions will be asked? How many senior managers will be asked to rate the team's performance and, again, on what dimensions? Different levels may be selected for different parts of the data collection process; for example the Team Innovation Questionnaire in this chapter is designed for use with both team leaders and other line managers.

5   *Select and train observers/interviewers.*   In order for information to be reliable, it is important that those who are responsible for collecting it, whether they are selected team members, team leaders or external specialists, receive training in the use of the evaluation tools and have enough information about the overall process to answer questions from team members. If you are in doubt about how best to manage the evaluation process, one alternative is to involve outside consultants who are skilled in this area. Chartered occupational psychologists are trained in these domains and will be able to offer help. The British Psychological Society keeps a register that will enable you to identify appropriately trained psychologists working in the United Kingdom.

6   *Carry out the evaluation activity.*   This should be done in a way that does not eat dramatically into people's time and into the time of the team. Keeping the evaluation activity proportionate to the work of the team is vital. Too much performance measurement and evaluation can interfere with the work of the team – akin to repeatedly pulling up young plants to check on how healthy their root development is.

- Plan the process – it should take no more than four weeks,
- Identify who will administer the questionnaires,
- Identify who will conduct interviews,
- Identify the teams to be involved in the evaluation (they should be representative),
- Select team members to interview/administer questionnaires – all, a random selection of team members, or a representative group,
- Select team leaders to interview/administer questionnaires – all, a random selection of team members, or a representative group,
- Enter the data on a database,
- Identify who will analyse the data,
- Decide who will present data back to each team, to the ISG and to the top management team,
- Decide how the data will be presented e.g., written reports, verbal presentations, or charts/Powerpoint slides,
- Decide how often the evaluation process will be repeated.

7   *Analyse the data.*   The data should be carefully analysed. Single comments by one service receiver that go against those of many should be given their due weight. Quantitative or numerical data should be carefully analysed. Are differences in scores from one year to the next minor variations or do they represent major shifts? It may be useful to encourage the team as a whole to help in the analysis of the data so they can make sense of them in the context of their own work. Have someone or a group analyse the data from the questionnaires and the interviews. These should be people who have experience, not just in data management, but also in the analysis of questionnaire surveys. Make sure the analyses are geared towards answering the questions you want answered by the evaluation process. Also be sure those responsible for the data analyses are not people who may have a particular prejudice about the organization, and who may use the opportunity to present a rather biased picture of the data. Alternatively, employ outside consultants to help with this process.

8   *Feedback to team members and key stakeholders.*   The context of feedback should always be attempting to answer the questions: 'What can we learn from this and how can we improve our performance?' The feedback should be as clear and supportive as possible, while making clear where areas of difficulty exist. When data are fed back, it is also important to protect the reputation

and feelings of people within the organization who may be harmed by too frank an exposition of the data. What should not happen is that, as a result of insensitive feedback, relationships between team members, or between team members and team leaders, or between teams are harmed. The feedback should be a constructive and supportive mechanism for improving TBW, particularly emphasizing good practice and successes. Of course it should be used to identify areas of improvement also, but not at the expense of positive support and reinforcement. The clearer and more direct the data feedback the better. Those receiving the feedback should be able to understand the data and make their own interpretations. This then enables them to act on the feedback to improve TBW within the organization – and this is the whole point of the exercise.

9   *Plan for the next review.*   As a result of the evaluation, you may find that you need to adjust your key performance indicators. You will certainly have access to a large amount of information and experience to enhance the evaluation process as necessary. The benefit of regular reviews is that the team can monitor change over time and this is often more useful and revealing information than one-off evaluations.

6.2   QUESTIONNAIRES FOR EVALUATING TEAM FUNCTIONING AND PERFORMANCE

Teams can find a variety of ways to evaluate their functioning and performance but below (and in the CD accompanying this book) we offer some validated questionnaires to assist in the process. The performance criteria for each team will be specific to that team. As we stressed in earlier chapters, it is important for both the organization and the individual team members to articulate the aims of the team clearly, to describe performance indicators and to establish systems for providing feedback on performance of key tasks. The measurement of team outcomes should follow logically from this early work.

TEAM PERFORMANCE QUESTIONNAIRE

This measure is designed to assess the performance of teams. It is also helpful in identifying causes when a team is known to be underperforming. It measures the dimensions that are known significantly to affect a team's ability to achieve performance outcomes, that is:

- the existence of a *motivating task with effective feedback,*
- the availability of *adequate knowledge and skills* within the team,
- the quality of *interpersonal relationships,*
- the application of sufficient *effort,*
- the development of appropriate *task performance strategies,*
- overall *effectiveness.*

We recommend that the questionnaire be completed by all team members, and that feedback be given on a whole-team basis (see under 'Suggested interventions' below).

TEAM PERFORMANCE QUESTIONNAIRE

Listed below are a number of statements that could describe a work group or team. Indicate how strongly you agree or disagree with each statement as it applies to the team in which you currently work.

Try to be as objective as you can in deciding how accurately each statement describes your team, regardless of whether you like or dislike being a member of the team.

Write a number in the blank space beside each statement, based on the following scale:

Strongly disagree	Mostly disagree	Slightly disagree	Uncertain	Slightly agree	Mostly agree	Strongly agree
1	2	3	4	5	6	7

Team motivation

_____ 1 The work our team does is important and therefore motivating.

_____ 2 The team's task is challenging but achievable.

_____ 3 The team receives clear feedback on its performance.

Team composition

_____ 4 Our team is the right size and has the right mix of people.

_____ 5 Team members have the knowledge and skills they need.

_____ 6 Team members work well together.

Interpersonal relationships

_____ 7 People in this team get on well.

_____ 8 There is little destructive conflict in the team.

_____ 9 We all know what we have to do to make the team effective.

Effort

_____ 10 All team members work hard.

_____ 11 All team members are committed to the task.

_____ 12 Team members make an effort to achieve team objectives.

Appropriate strategy

_____ 13 The team develops appropriate strategies for getting the job done effectively.

_____ 14 We plan the team's work carefully.

_____ 15 We regularly review how the team should best perform its task.

Effectiveness

_____ 16 The team is regularly told it is productive.

_____ 17 Managers say our team's work is of high quality.

Suggested interventions

Scores will indicate areas of good and poor performance. Average scores of 5 or less in any area indicate a need for action to rectify some aspect of performance. Refer to Table 6.1 to identify which stage of the TBW process might help in developing your teams' performance.

TEAM AUTONOMY REVIEW

At any stage in a team's life, seeking team members' own assessment of the degree of discretion they are allowed in managing

Table 6.1 Suggested interventions for team performance

Area of concern	Intervention	References	Stages
Team motivation	Review team design	Task requirements	1,4
		Individual team design	1,4
Task feedback	Review processes	Performance reviews	2
		Reward systems	2
Team composition/adequate skills and knowledge	Review team composition	Individual team design	1,4
		Selecting for teamworking	2
		Effects of diversity	2
	Evaluate training needs	Plan training provision	3
	Team process review	Knowledge, skills and abilities	3
		Team roles	4
	External coaching/facilitation for the team	Process support systems	2
Interpersonal relationships	Training for team leaders and/or team members	Conflict resolution	4
		Decision making	4
		Constructive controversy	4
	Team communications review	Effective team communications	4
Effort	Review task motivation	Task requirement survey	4
	Team leader training	Developing a team vision	3
Appropriate strategy	Role clarification	Role clarification and negotiation	4
	Team leader and/or team member training	Team leader training (+ Stage 6 for team members?)	3
Effectiveness	Review low score areas above	Developing a team vision	4
	Clarify team vision and team member objectives	Individual objective setting	6

their goal outcomes and working methods can produce powerful – and sometimes surprising – results. Senior managers may find that they need to clarify boundaries or areas of autonomy which are not reflected in how the team works.

Particularly during the implementation stages of TBW, it is important to monitor the degree to which teams are moving towards autonomy of action and decision making and away from external direction. Many organizations have experienced difficulty in introducing autonomous teams where middle and first-line managers have been unable to move away from old patterns of working. Team members may also take some time to adjust to new responsibilities. Over time, and particularly when there is a crisis, the team may slip back into expectations of external direction rather than exercising its newly established powers of self-direction.

The Team Autonomy Review (reproduced for copying on the accompanying CD) is a helpful tool for monitoring the development of team autonomy over time. We have found that, during the early life of TBW within an organization, there is an ideal level of autonomy for each organization and each team. This is dependent upon several factors:

- the stage of development of TBW within the organization,
- the stage of development of the team being monitored,
- the definition of 'autonomy' for this type of team in this particular organization.

The Team Autonomy Review questionnaire may therefore be used in one of two ways:

1 To measure the organization's teams against a model of a fully autonomous, self-directing team (which would respond 'always' for every question in the questionnaire below). In this case, administer the questionnaire as directed in the text below.
2 As the basis for designing a tool which monitors the development of teams against a vision of autonomous working teams in your organization. In this case, identify the areas in which teams are required to exercise autonomy and establish minimum scores against which to monitor progress.

The questionnaire should be completed by the most senior manager responsible for the area in which the team works, by the team leader and by team members. The manager should note what he or she believes should be happening in the decision-making situations described. This will enable comparison with team leader and team member responses at the end of the review.

TEAM AUTONOMY REVIEW QUESTIONNAIRE

	Never	Sometimes	Frequently	Always

1 The team decides its own goals in terms of:
a) quantity: i.e. how much it is expected to produce and under what financial conditions
b) quality: the standards which are to be expected in terms of team outputs.

2 The team decides:
a) where to work
b) when to work: i.e. the number of hours worked by the team as a whole, or when individual members can leave or work overtime
c) in what other activities it wishes to engage: i.e. the team can interrupt its activity to do other things.

3 The team decides on methods of production.

4 The team decides on internal distribution of tasks.

5 The team decides on its membership: i.e. it can choose new members and exclude undesired members.

6 The team decides if it wishes to have a leader to coordinate activity

within the team and
selects the leader.

7 The team decides if it
   wishes to have a person
   to represent the team
   externally and selects
   that person.

8 Individual members of
   the team decide how to
   carry out their own tasks.

Scoring is as follows:

Never = 0; Sometimes = 1; Frequently = 2; Always = 3

The minimum score for a team is therefore 0 and the maximum is 33. Clearly no team should score 0. The minimum score for any team, even a newly formed one, should be 5. The aim should be for all teams to move progressively towards scores in the high 20s (28, 29) or even into the 30s. Scores above 25 suggest teams that are working highly autonomously, and those scoring 30 and over are achieving the ideal of autonomous teamworking (assuming they are also performing effectively).

TEAM CLIMATE INVENTORY (TCI)

The TCI is widely used to measure team climate and processes. We recommend that it should be included in any comprehensive survey of teamworking. It is also useful for working with specific team problems in new and established teams. It measures team vision, participation, task orientation, interaction and support for innovation. It is an excellent diagnostic tool for evaluating teamworking in organizations.

The TCI was developed by Neil Anderson and Michael West, and is a copyrighted commercial instrument with computer-based scoring and reports, available from ASE, Darville House, 2 Oxford Road East, Windsor, Berkshire SL4 1DF, UK. This questionnaire has been used in organizations throughout the world and translated into many different languages. It provides a rigorous way of assessing the processes in a team and offers a large database of norms for the functioning of teams against which to compare your own team's functioning. The TCI has 44 items and measures a number of subdimensions including clarity of, and commitment to, team objectives, information sharing, interaction frequency, influence over decision making, task orientation, and support for innovation. A sample of items is given below.

TEAM CLIMATE INVENTORY

1 Participation in the team
This part concerns how much participation there is in your team. Please tick the most appropriate response to you for each question.

To what extent do you agree with the following?

	Strongly disagree	Disagree	Neither agree nor disagree	Agree	Strongly agree
3 We have a 'we are in it together' attitude.	☐	☐	☐	☐	☐
5 People keep each other informed about work-related issues in the team.	☐	☐	☐	☐	☐
6 People feel understood and accepted by each other.	☐	☐	☐	☐	☐
9 There are real attempts to share information throughout the team.	☐	☐	☐	☐	☐
13 There is a lot of give and take.	☐	☐	☐	☐	☐
14 We keep in touch with each other as a team.	☐	☐	☐	☐	☐

2 Support for new ideas
This part deals with attitudes towards change in your team. Please indicate how strongly you agree or disagree with each of the following statements as a description of your team by ticking the appropriate box.

To what extent do you agree with the following?

	Strongly disagree	Disagree	Neither agree nor disagree	Agree	Strongly agree
1 This team is always moving toward the development of new answers.	☐	☐	☐	☐	☐
3 This team is open and responsive to change.	☐	☐	☐	☐	☐
5 People in this team are always searching for fresh, new ways of looking at problems.	☐	☐	☐	☐	☐
9 Members of the team provide and share resources to help in the application of new ideas.	☐	☐	☐	☐	☐
10 Team members provide practical support for new ideas and their application.	☐	☐	☐	☐	☐

3 Team Objectives

The following statements concern your understanding of your team's objectives. Tick the appropriate box to indicate how far each statement describes your team.

	Not at all		Somewhat		Completely		
1 How clear are you about what your team's objectives are?	☐	☐	☐	☐	☐	☐	☐
3 How far are you in agreement with these objectives?	☐	☐	☐	☐	☐	☐	☐

4 To what extent do
you think other team
members agree with
these objectives?   □ □ □ □ □ □ □
11 To what extent do
you think members
of your team are
committed to these
objectives?   □ □ □ □ □ □ □

4 Task Style
The questions below concern how you feel the team monitors and appraises the work it does. Consider to what extent each of the following questions describes your team. Please tick the box under the response which you think best describes your team.

	To a very little extent	To some extent	To a very great extent

1 Do your team
colleagues provide
useful ideas and
practical help to
enable you to do the
job to the best of
your ability?   □ □ □ □ □ □ □
3 Are team members
prepared to question
the basis of what the
team is doing?   □ □ □ □ □ □ □
4 Does the team critically
appraise potential
weaknesses in what
it is doing in order to
achieve the best
possible outcome?   □ □ □ □ □ □ □
5 Do members of the
team build on each
other's ideas in order
to achieve the highest
possible standards
of performance?   □ □ □ □ □ □ □

TEAM PROCESS QUESTIONNAIRE (TPQ)

This measure (reproduced for copying on the accompanying CD) is an alternative to the TCI described above. It has far fewer items (only 16) and provides a useful measure of the following aspects of team functioning:

- Clarity of team objectives,
- Participation in the team,
- Interpersonal safety and support in the team,
- Constructive debate,
- Support for innovation.

To administer the questionnaire, we recommend you give it to all members of teams to complete. If this is impractical have three randomly selected members complete the questionnaire. Take an average of the scores of those who have completed the questionnaire. Overall, a minimum score of 48 is desirable for a reasonably well-functioning team. But the ideal is to aim for scores of between 70 and 80. By analysing subsets of items it is possible to identify particular areas of strength and weakness within teams:

Items 1–3   Clarity of and commitment to team objectives,
Items 4–7   Level of participation in the team,
Items 8–10   Level of support and safety in the team,
Items 11–13   Constructive debate within the team,
Items 14–16   Support for innovation.

It is also possible to examine the data for each team and see if there are areas where team members disagree markedly in their evaluations of the team's functioning. If there are, this can be a useful basis for discussion within the team. In any event, the team should have a discussion about the data on its functioning and consider ways of reinforcing its effective functioning and improving areas of ineffective functioning. The team leader, the change manager, a member of the HRM department or an external consultant can facilitate this process.

TEAM PROCESS QUESTIONNAIRE

Response scale

	Very inaccurate description	Inaccurate description	Somewhat accurate	Accurate description	Very accurate description
	1	2	3	4	5

1 In this team we are clear about what we are trying to achieve.

2 Team members are committed to achieving the team's objectives.

3 We agree in the team about what are our team objectives.

4 We meet together sufficiently frequently to ensure effective communication and cooperation.

5 Everyone in the team contributes to decision making.

6 We all influence the final decisions made in the team.

7 We are careful to keep each other informed about work issues.

8 There is a feeling of trust and safety in this team.

9 We work supportively together to get the job done.

10 We know we can rely on one another in this team.

11 We can safely discuss errors and mistakes in the team.

12 We have lively debates about how best to do the work.

13 There is a climate of constructive criticism in this team.

14 We support each other in ideas for new and improved ways of doing the team's work.

15 We are enthusiastic about innovation in this team.

16 People in the team are quick to offer help to try out new ways of doing things.

TEAM INNOVATION QUESTIONNAIRE

One of the main reasons organizations give for moving to TBW is the need for increased innovation in response to market pressures for new products, increased quality and reduced costs. Team innovation will be present to a greater or lesser degree in two areas:

- *technical innovations*: the introduction and development of new product ideas,
- *process innovations*: the introduction of new ways of working within the team.

The Team Innovation Questionnaire (reproduced for copying on the accompanying CD) assesses the comparative levels of innovation between similar work teams. It can also be used to monitor the development of innovative practices against an organizationally established 'target' for innovation in an individual team or type of teams. In the latter case the organization will need to identify what level of innovation it requires from the team by establishing an 'ideal team score' against which teams will be monitored. The third section of the questionnaire asks about the source of the ideas that are implemented by the team. This information will enable you to identify whether a team is intrinsically an innovative team or one that generally implements ideas generated from other sources. The questionnaire should be completed by team leaders or those who are external to the team but have the opportunity to observe its work closely.

TEAM INNOVATION QUESTIONNAIRE

Section One
Assess the quantity of ideas that are produced by this team in comparison to other similar teams. Please use the blank space beside each statement to indicate your assessment based on the following scale:

1	2	3	4	5
Many fewer than average	Fewer than average	Average	A few more than average	Many more than average

Compared with other similar teams, how many new ideas does this team come up with in terms of:

1 New products, technology or services
2 New elements in the process of
   producing products or services
3 New elements in the operations that
   produce products and services
4 New technology that will increase the
   efficiency with which the product or
   service is produced
5 New procedures that are related to
   communication between team members
6 New structures within the workforce or team
7 New roles for team members
8 New rules which are applied to the way
   in which team members conduct the task

Section Two

Assess the quality of ideas produced by this team in comparison to other similar teams. Please use the blank space beside each statement to indicate your assessment based on the following scale:

1	2	3	4	5
Very low	**Low**	**Average**	**High**	**Very high**

Compared with other similar teams, what is the quality of the ideas that are implemented by this team in terms of:

 9 New products, technology or services
10 New elements in the process of producing
    products or services
11 New elements in the operations that produce
 ˙ products and services
12 New technology that will increase the
    efficiency with which the product or
    service is produced
13 New procedures that are related to
    communication between team members
14 New structures within the workforce or team
15 New roles for team members
16 New rules which are applied to the way
    in which team members conduct the task

Section Three

To what extent does the team develop the following types of innovation? Please indicate by circling the appropriate response.

	Very little	Somewhat		A great deal	
Ideas that are adopted from other teams/organizations	1	2	3	4	5
Ideas that are original to this team	1	2	3	4	5
Ideas that are enforced by senior people outside the team	1	2	3	4	5
Ideas that are a result of changes within the organization	1	2	3	4	5
Ideas that are prompted by customer/client suggestions	1	2	3	4	5
Ideas that are prompted by the team leader or other line management	1	2	3	4	5

The questionnaire should be scored by summing the responses for each section. An ideal score for a team is 32 and over for both Sections 1 and 2, and 25 and over for section 3. Obviously teams should strive to maximize their scores. A minimally acceptable score on Sections 1 and 2 is 24 and on Section 3 is 18. Where the scores are very low, consider ways of promoting creativity and innovation (see, e.g., West, 1997).

TEAM MEMBER INNOVATION QUESTIONNAIRE

This questionnaire (reproduced for copying in the accompanying CD) allows team members to reflect upon how innovative they are in their work. The results from this measure are useful as a basis for discussion within the team regarding the team's ability to innovate effectively. You may also find it helpful to compare the perception of team members gained from this questionnaire with those of team leaders or external observers elicited from the Team Innovation Questionnaire to identify areas of strength and weakness in the team's development.

TEAM MEMBER INNOVA-TION QUESTIONNAIRE

The following questions explore your feelings about innovation and change at work. How far do you agree or disagree with the following statements? Please place a number in the blank space next to each statement based on the following scale:

1	2	3	4	5
Strongly disagree	**Disagree**	**Not sure**	**Agree**	**Strongly agree**

I try to introduce improved methods of doing things at work.

I have ideas which significantly improve the way the job is done.

I suggest new working methods to the people I work with.

I contribute to changes in the way my team works.

I am receptive to new ideas which I can use to improve things at work.

Total score

Interpretation of the Team Member Innovation Questionnaire

Scores of over 19 suggest that the individual is likely to produce creative ideas. The overall propensity for teams to be creative and innovative in the way in which they work can be predicted by averaging the scores on this measure for all team members. The number of creative ideas produced will be increased by the presence of one highly creative individual within a team. The team's implementation of these ideas, however, will be influenced by the status which that particular team member holds within the team.

TEAM MEMBER SATISFACTION QUESTIONNAIRE

Measures of satisfaction highlight the team's ability to provide for its individual members:

- satisfaction in the work that they carry out,
- a supportive social climate,
- the opportunity for personal growth and development.

The Team Member Satisfaction Questionnaire (reproduced for copying in the accompanying CD) is designed to survey team members' attitudes to each of these areas as they relate to their primary work team. In order to score it, simply sum the totals for each individual.

Those scoring 40 and below are not happy in their teamwork and are less likely to be creative and cooperative as a consequence. It is important for the team leader or for the team as a whole to initiate a discussion about how both individual and team satisfaction and motivation could be improved. Those scoring between 40 and 60 are similarly less than optimally satisfied in their work and this could affect the team's functioning overall. Again, it would be useful (though rather less urgent) for the team leader, or indeed all team members, to discuss ways of promoting satisfaction and motivation within the team.

FOCUS GROUP INTERVIEWS

It is useful to augment questionnaire-based surveys with other means of eliciting information about the way in which teams are working, such as focus groups and interviews. Below, and on the accompanying CD, are some questions (adapted from Hackman, 1990) that could be used in focus group interviews with a team.

Sample interview questions

- What are the team's main objectives?
- Do all members of the team get really involved in work on the team task, and try especially hard to do a good job on it?
- Do the members of the team have the appropriate combinations of knowledge or skills to accomplish the team task?
- Is the team either too large or too small for what it has to accomplish?
- How efficient is the team – is it very clear what people expect each other to do, and does everybody do what is expected of them?
- Does your team deliberately take some time away from the task work to consider new or better ways of proceeding with the work?

TEAM MEMBER SATISFACTION QUESTIONNAIRE

Circle the number that best describes how satisfied you are with each feature of your current job or the team in which you primarily work:

	Very dissatisfied	Moderately dissatisfied	Not sure	Moderately satisfied	Very satisfied
1 The freedom to choose your own method of working	1	2	3	4	5
2 The recognition you receive from colleagues for your contribution to the team	1	2	3	4	5
3 The opportunity for career progression	1	2	3	4	5
4 The amount of responsibility you are given	1	2	3	4	5
5 The support you receive from team colleagues	1	2	3	4	5
6 The opportunity to use your skills and knowledge	1	2	3	4	5
7 The way in which conflicts are resolved	1	2	3	4	5
8 The availability of constructive feedback regarding the work that you do	1	2	3	4	5
9 The attention paid to suggestions you make	1	2	3	4	5
10 The amount of variety in your job	1	2	3	4	5
11 The opportunities you have to influence decision making	1	2	3	4	5
12 The amount of training you receive	1	2	3	4	5
13 The availability of new tasks which enable you to develop new skills	1	2	3	4	5
14 The opportunity to discuss work-related problems in an open manner	1	2	3	4	5
15 The availability of different team roles which you can undertake	1	2	3	4	5

- How good is communication between team members?
- Does the team get some kind of special reward or recognition from management when it performs particularly well?
- Does the team ever fail to meet some performance goal or target, and if so why?
- When your team needs some special training or consultation about how to do certain parts of the task, do they get it?
- Does the team get told the things you need to know about task requirements or performance objectives?
- Do managers give your team ideas or assistance that helps members work together better as a team?
- Do all team members get involved in making team decisions?
- Does the team leader go out of his or her way to consult with you in advance about a decision that would affect your team or its work?
- Does the team have the resources it needs?
- Does the work of the team suffer because of problems with some other team (either within or outside the organization)?
- Does the team's performance exceed the standards or expectations of the people who review your work?
- Do relationships within the team get so bad that they interfere with the members' ability to work together effectively on the task?
- Overall, what would you say was the single 'best thing' about this team?
- Overall, what would you say was the single 'worst thing' about it?

6.3 SUSTAINING AND IMPROVING PERFORMANCE: ENCOURAGING REFLEXIVITY

Teams that operate in uncertain, challenging environments will be more effective to the extent that they attend to and reflect upon their objectives, strategies, processes and their organizational and wider environments; plan to make appropriate changes on the basis of these reflections; and make changes accordingly. They will also facilitate creativity and skill development among team members. Moreover such 'reflexive' teams will stimulate innovation or even revolution in their organizations by negotiating, challenging and influencing organizational goals, policies

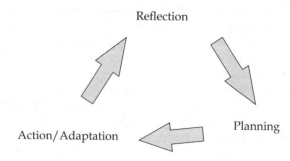

Figure 6.1   The reflexivity cycle

and practices. What we propose is that teams can best support and improve their performance by learning about their functioning on an ongoing basis rather than bringing in outside consultants or going away on repeated team-building courses. Teams that take time out to reflect on what it is they are trying to do and how they are going about it are simply much more effective and more innovative than those that do not. Team reflection, planning and action lead to improving performance and high levels of innovation.

In reflexive teams, members reflect, plan and act in relation to their team objectives by considering the appropriateness of those objectives in relation to team members' and stakeholders' objectives, the clarity of their objectives, the value to stakeholders and to team members, and the team's commitment to them. In such teams, members draw attention to and focus upon objectives and processes of team meetings. Reflexive teams also give attention to team strategies or plans for achieving goals, including consideration of their detail, clarity and value; what alternatives might be considered; the timescale; and their likely effectiveness. Timescales might be long-term (five or ten years ahead), medium-term (the next three to six months or one year), or short-term (immediate in relation to the meeting or task). This will depend upon the timescale of the task and the tenure of the team – project teams may have a lifetime of only six months, so the timescale of their planning will be foreshortened.

Reflexive teams will also consider, plan and act in order to improve team processes, including decision making in the team; leadership – including whether it is distributed or invested in one person, and whether it is predominantly transformational or transactional in style; communication; frequency and type of interaction between members (including electronically mediated interactions such as e-mail and voice mail); recruitment and selection; management of controversy and conflict within the team; methods of monitoring performance; ways of seeking and responding to feedback; support for innovation in the team; and, of course, team effectiveness.

Nonreflexive teams can be identified by their failure to consider and review their objectives, strategies, processes and environments, and by a tendency to react to the situation that exists at the moment. This is in contrast to reflexive teams, which plan strategies ahead and actively structure the situation, including seeking feedback. Nonreflexive teams will exhibit defensiveness against awareness of team processes, strategy planning and change, and be recalcitrant in their willingness to review and reflect on their experience and objectives.

WHAT INITIATES REFLEXIVITY?

When teams 'turn back on themselves' and examine their objectives, team processes and strategies, their organizations and their environments, discrepancies between actual and desired circumstances are almost always revealed, and this can be uncomfortable. As a consequence of reflection or problem identification, the team experiences anxiety and uncertainty, members become increasingly aroused, and thus the motivation to reflect may be reduced. Because reflection often involves recognizing discrepancies between real and ideal circumstances, then it is unlikely to arise spontaneously within many teams. Moreover, reflection may demand change in action but individuals in organizations are chronically resistant to change. Therefore, team reflexivity is unlikely to arise naturally, but would have to be induced by leadership facilitation.

To nurture reflexivity in teams requires styles and patterns of *leadership* which create the conditions for exploration, experimentation and risk taking, in developing shared commitment to reflecting on, and questioning, team and organizational objectives, strategies and processes. Such a team leader will constantly ask: 'What can we learn from this?' Such leadership processes are most likely to be found in 'transformational leaders' – those who concentrate their efforts on longer term goals, emphasize a vision and inspire team members to pursue the vision, change organizations to suit the vision rather than working within existing systems, and coach followers to take responsibility for their and fellow team members' development.

Team member changes provide an opportunity for reflection, including reflection on the composition of the team and on team processes and practices which surprise the newcomer. Newcomers can also share experiences of good practices in other teams which the team could import to learn about. Characteristically, teams 'socialize' newcomers as quickly as possible, shaping them to accept and comply with team norms. Reflexive groups may be more inclined to seek newcomers' reactions to the team's ways of working and encourage the newcomer to share experiences of successful team processes and strategies from his or her previous work experience. Interestingly, the longer teams have been together, the less they communicate with key information sources, scan the environment, and communicate within the team and with other organizational divisions and external professions. Team longevity is associated with a tendency to ignore and become increasingly isolated from sources that provide the most critical kinds of feedback, evaluation and information. This suggests that without optimal changes in membership and function, teams may become less reflexive over time.

Errors and failures in team functioning offer critically important opportunities for reflection and have the potential to stimulate teams to reflect on the processes or assumptions which lead to them. A key indicator is the reaction of teams to errors. In non-reflexive teams, errors are unlikely to be acknowledged or dealt with. In reflexive teams errors are seen as opportunities to reflect on and learn about team functioning. In a revealing example of this, Edmondson (1996) describes a study in which nursing teams with effective team leaders and good quality team functioning were *more* likely to report adverse drug episodes in hospitals – giving the wrong drug or the wrong dose of the correct drug. Such teams create a climate of openness, which facilitates discussion of, and learning from, errors. For example, team members may reflect upon what it is about the team's way of working that enabled the error to occur. Errors are thus seen as opportunities for growth rather than events to be ignored and glossed over or hastily corrected. Nonreflexive teams, in contrast, will tend to deny errors or give up on long-term planning and fall back upon short-term strategies at times of crises.

Few teams use *success* as a cue for reflection and action. And yet dwelling on the reasons why the team succeeded represents a very good opportunity for reflection and action. Simply celebrating success wastes the potential for learning which success offers. Nonreflexive teams are likely to accept successes unquestioningly; teams high in reflexivity are more likely to analyse and consider the causes of success.

When *intrateam conflicts* occur, teams characterized by high levels of task reflexivity are more likely to respond by reflecting on and learning about the underlying processes and causes of the conflict. In particular there is a need to reflect on the value of the conflict – was it conflict that was productive in enabling the team as a whole to achieve its objectives better? Were good conflict management processes employed? How could the benefits and disadvantages of the conflict be respectively gained and avoided in the future?

Difficulties over time allocation present further opportunities for reflection. When group members experience work overload, it suggests a need to reflect upon objectives and priorities. Many teams in health care contexts find themselves trapped in a vicious cycle of work overload, inhibiting them from taking time out to determine priorities, based on the health needs of their client groups. This results in increasing work demands and ever more limited capacity for reflection. Awareness of the experience of overwork should prompt teams to reflect upon team functioning and how and why external demands are swamping intelligent processes of strategy development, prioritizing and resource allocation.

Difficulties in synchronizing team member activities (e.g. to arrange meetings) suggest a need for reflection to discuss how team or individual processes are inhibiting effective collaboration, cooperation and synchrony. When team members are unable to synchronize time use, in order to meet or to complete a team task effectively, it is often because team functioning is ineffective in some area. Individual objectives may be taking precedence over the team task, or the team task is inadequately specified. Awareness of the difficulties of synchronizing time and tasks among team members provides an important opportunity for reflection on team functioning.

Interruptions, and particularly conflicts, crises, shocks, surprises, obstacles and changes, create moments of potential attention or awareness, where the group can step back from involvement in task-related issues and take the opportunity to attend to team, organizational or environmental issues. Interruptions to the team's work by senior managers or other teams can lead to reflection and action, in relation to the appropriateness of these interruptions, or the team's need to adapt effectively to such discontinuities. Unpredictable outside events can interfere with the team's functioning and thus offer another opportunity for reflection about its failure to predict or adapt to such perturbations, and what this implies. Technical interruptions due to machine breakdown, for example, and organizational problems such as lack of supplies, provide further opportunities for reflection. What causes the machine breakdown, or what is ineffective in organizational systems that leads to supplies not being available when needed?

Feedback seeking provides learning opportunities and opportunities for reflection stimulated by the perceptions and reactions of those outside the team, particularly stakeholders. The concept of feedback seeking and feedback use is widely applied in studying individual work behaviour, but it has clear applicability also to the development of reflexivity in groups. Teams which process performance feedback in a self-serving, defensive manner, rather than reflecting on performance issues, are likely to be low in reflexivity (and consequently low in performance). How much feedback teams seek is another useful indicator of reflexivity, since it suggests that a team is sufficiently open in its interpretation of its world and functioning to value external feedback.

Organizational change can trigger a team to consider the support provided by the organization, in terms of clarity of direction, education and communication systems, rewards systems, process assistance and integration devices. Moreover, organizational change may cause the team to reflect on and challenge organizational objectives, policies and practices as well as its relationship with the wider community and environment of which it is a part.

There are many opportunities for teams to be reflexive in their functioning but, in most cases, coaching is required to enable members to develop this capability or competence. Reflexivity must be part of the threads of the day-to-day texture of the team's work experience and part of the broad pattern of its functioning over time, if it is to be sustained. Leadership is a vital facilitating process to enable teams to overcome the natural inertia and barriers against reflection, planning and adaptation, especially since some elements of the process will be aversive. This requires leadership which enables processes of reflexivity to occur by creating a sufficiently safe and learning-oriented environment.

Many 'teams' in organizations do not have sufficient member interdependence, clear objectives, and appropriate team task performance feedback necessary for minimally effective team performance. Indeed, team or team functioning in a wide variety of organizational settings appears to be rather primitive. Consequently, it is suggested that processes of task reflexivity in team functioning require considerable practical development if the potential of work teams is to be realized. Teams should therefore be encouraged to reflect on their functioning and performance in the following domains of activity, during 'away days', in team meetings and during the course of performing:

- *Team objectives*, e.g. their appropriateness, clarity, value to stakeholders and to team members, and the team's commitment to them, as well as objectives in team meetings;
- *Team strategies or plans for achieving goals*, e.g. their detail, clarity, value, alternatives, time span, effectiveness;
- *Team processes*, e.g. decision making, leadership, communication, interaction frequency, recruitment and selection, controversy, monitoring, feedback, processes in meetings, self-appraisal, support for innovation, effectiveness;
- *Organization*, e.g. goals, practices, policies, supports for the team, information and communication systems, reward systems, appraisal systems, feedback on performance, intra-organization linkages, cross-team collaboration, wider social influence, environmental impacts.

Below is a measure of reflexivity in teams (reproduced for copying on the accompanying CD) that has been used with teams in a wide variety of settings. It provides a clear indication of the level of reflexivity of a team and therefore of the extent to which it will sustain good performance, improve its performance and exhibit high levels of creativity and innovation.

THE TEAM REFLEXIVITY QUESTIONNAIRE

To measure levels of reflexivity in a team, ask all team members to complete this questionnaire without consulting each other about the answers. Reverse the scores for items 5 and 8 (i.e., 1 = 7, 2 = 6, 3 = 5, 4 = 4). Add the scores. Divide both totals by the number of people completing the questionnaire. At the bottom of this box are values against which you can determine whether your team's scores are high, low or average compared with the scores of other teams. *Indicate how far each statement is an accurate or inaccurate description of your team by writing a number in the box beside each statement, based on the following scale of 1 to 7:*

Very inaccurate						Very accurate
1	2	3	4	5	6	7

Task reflexivity

1   The team often reviews its objectives.   ☐
2   We regularly discuss whether the team
    is working effectively together.   ☐
3   The methods used by the team to
    get the job done are often discussed.   ☐
4   In this team we modify our objectives
    in light of changing circumstances.   ☐
5   Team strategies are rarely changed.   ☐
6   How well we communicate information
    is often discussed.   ☐
7   This team often reviews its approach
    to getting the job done.   ☐
8   The way decisions are made in this
    team is rarely altered.   ☐

Total score   ☐

High scores   42–56
Average scores   34–41
Low scores   8–33

Where the scores are medium and low refer to the information given under 'What initiates reflexivity' above for guidance.

What this book does suggest is that teams, like individuals, have to reflect upon their functioning and adapt in ways which are appropriate to their changing circumstances. Such an orientation requires:

* intelligent scanning of the environment,
* awareness of the functioning of the team,
* flexibility or readiness to change,

- tolerance of ambiguity and difference within the team,
- a preparedness to accept uncertainty as change occurs.

One reason why simple prescriptions cannot be offered for effective team work is that teams operate in varied organizational settings – as diverse as multinational oil companies, voluntary organizations, health care organizations and religious institutions. While team effectiveness is an important issue in all, the people who constitute these teams are likely to differ in personality and background.

Even within organizations teams differ markedly. Increasingly within Europe, for example, teams are constituted from people who have different cultural backgrounds. In some organizations teams may span national boundaries, including perhaps members located in a number of different nation states, all of whom are required to work effectively together. Moreover, changes in work patterns such as part-time, flexitime, contract and home working all add further mixes to the heterogeneity of teams. As teams become more diverse in their constitution and functioning, team members must learn to reflect upon, and intelligently adapt to, their constantly changing circumstances in order to be effective. This means that evaluation, reflection, planning and action should be fundamental and taken-for-granted ways of working in teams. This, after all, is what the most successful sports teams have always done. Finally, we turn to an evaluation of the effects that TBW has upon the organization as a whole, and how this can be evaluated.

REFERENCES AND FURTHER READING

Agrell, A., & Gustafson R. (1994). The Team Climate Inventory (TCI) and group innovation: A psychometric test on a Swedish sample of work groups. *Journal of Occupational and Organizational Psychology*, 67: 143–51.

Anderson, N., & West, M.A. (1996). The Team Climate Inventory: Development of the TCI and its applications in teambuilding for innovativeness. *European Journal of Work and Organizational Psychology*, 5, 1: 53–66.

Anderson, N., & West, M.A. (1998). Measuring climate for work group innovation: Development and validation of the team climate inventory. *Journal of Organizational Behaviour*, 19: 235–58.

Anderson, N.R., and West, M.A., (2000). *The Team Climate Inventory: Manual and User's Guide*. Windsor, UK: ASE Press.

Carter, S.M., & West, M.A. (1998). Reflexivity, effectiveness and mental health in BBC-TV production teams. *Small Group Research*, 29, 5: 583–601

Cordery, J.L. (1996). Autonomous work groups. In M.A. West (ed.), *The Handbook of Work Group Psychology*. Chichester, UK: Wiley, pp. 225–46.

Edmondson, A.C. (1996). Learning from mistakes is easier said than done: Group and organizational influences on the detection and correction of human error. *Journal of Applied Behavioral Science*, 32, 1: 5–28.

Hackman, J.R. (ed.) (1990). *Groups That Work (and Those That Don't): Creating Conditions for Effective Teamwork*. San Francisco: Jossey Bass.

Schön, D.A. (1983). *The Reflective Practitioner: How Professionals Think in Action*. New York: Basic Books.

Schön, D.A. (1994). Teaching artistry through reflection-in-action. In H. Tsoukas (ed.), *New Thinking in Organizational Behaviour*. Oxford: Butterworth-Heinmann, pp. 235–49.

Tjosvold, D. (1991). *Team Organization: An Enduring Competitive Advantage*. Chichester, UK: Wiley.

West, M.A. (1994). *Effective Teamwork*. Leicester, UK: British Psychological Society Books.

West, M.A. (1997). *Developing Creativity in Organizations*. Leicester, UK: British Psychological Society Books/Oxford: Blackwell.

West, M.A. (2000). Reflexivity, revolution, and innovation in work teams. In M.M. Beyerlein, D.A. Johnson and S.T. Beyerlein (eds.), *Product Development Teams*. Stamford, CT: JAI Press, pp. 1–29.

7

ORGANIZATION-LEVEL ASSESSMENT

KEY AIMS

- Establish measurement criteria for
  - team contribution to the organization,
  - the success of the introduction of team-based working (TBW),
- Evaluate and provide feedback on the implementation of TBW,
- Establish procedures to continuously review the functioning of the organization.

KEY TASKS

- To measure financial performance or overall goal achievement and the contribution of TBW,
- To measure change in customer or service receiver satisfaction and the contribution of TBW to this change,
- To measure business processes and the contribution of TBW to their development,
- To monitor organizational innovation and the contribution of TBW to innovation,
- To monitor intergroup collaboration and cooperation or hostility and conflict,

- To initiate regular reviews of organizational functioning and effectiveness and the role of TBW in this.

KEY PEOPLE

- The top management team,
- The implementation steering group (ISG),
- All team leaders and team members.

The most important question is not whether the teams are functioning as they should but whether team-based organizing is producing the results it was intended to. Whether the task is catching wildebeest on the savannah, saving lives in hospitals in Johannesburg, teaching schoolchildren how to make sense of their worlds and be productive members of society in India, or making good profits as an aluminium smelting company in Norway, the value of team-based organizing is in its contributions to the achievement of the organization's or the community's goals.

The final step in TBW involves identifying the key organizational indicators of effectiveness and measuring the contribution of team-based organizing to these domains of effectiveness. Below, we consider various areas of effectiveness and associated measures, including goal achievement, customer satisfaction, employee development, innovation and intergroup or interdepartmental collaboration.

One approach we recommend to examining organizational effectiveness is based on Robert Kaplan and David Norton's Balanced Scorecard (Kaplan & Norton, 1998). The Balanced Scorecard provides a comprehensive framework that translates an organization's vision and strategy into a coherent set of performance measures. The Balanced Scorecard approach is particularly valuable for assessing organizational performance since it incorporates four major perspectives on organizational effectiveness. These perspectives are:

- Financial performance or goal achievement,
- Customer or service receiver satisfaction,
- Internal efficiency or business processes,
- Innovation, including employee growth and learning.

We consider the contribution of team-based organizing to each of these domains below.

7.1 GOAL ACHIEVEMENT OR FINANCIAL PERFORMANCE

Team-based organizing should contribute to improvements in performance in relation to the core goals of the organization. In the case of commercial companies, this will usually include financial performance (productivity or profitability figures); for schools it would include the academic performance of the pupils; for hospitals it might be patient mortality or recovery from illness. The question you need to ask is 'How is team-based organizing contributing directly to improved financial performance or to the attainment of organizational goals?'; the subsidiary question is 'How can this contribution be further enhanced?' For example, in one company we worked in, production teams succeeded in reducing product lead time (the time from receiving an order from a customer to the time when the order content was delivered to the customer) by a factor of 10. An average 60 days was reduced to an average six with a consequent increase in customer loyalty and demand, and thereby financial performance. Moreover, the reduction in lead times was largely achieved by building in efficient business processes, which in turn reduced costs of production dramatically. The team were given a share of the resulting profits which motivated their further commitment to team working and to innovation.

7.2 CUSTOMER OR SERVICE RECEIVER PERSPECTIVES

Linked to goal achievement is the perspective of the consumer or service receiver on the effectiveness of the organization. These perspectives may not be perfectly aligned with financial performance, particularly in the long term. A company may make short-term profits by offering very poor service. For example, the Swedish home furnishings company, IKEA, has frequently been criticized for achieving low prices and high profit by sacrificing customer service. A school may achieve excellent academic results but at the cost of children's enjoyment of their school years and this may dissuade parents from sending their younger children to the school. If the reputation of a hospital is excellent but the waiting time for operations is an average of two years, the consumer perspective is likely not to be coloured with a golden hue. Similarly, a car manufacturer may produce wonderfully efficient and reliable cars but if delivery time is months rather than weeks, consumers are unlikely to wait.

In this domain too, it is important to ask the questions, 'How is team-based organizing contributing to more positive customer perspectives?' and 'How can it do this more effectively?' Product quality and on-time delivery should be enhanced by team-based organizing. We have already given the example above of teams reducing product lead time. In another manufacturing organization we worked with, the CEO devolved responsibility for customer liaison directly to the shop floor teams. Consequently, customers negotiated their orders (for packaging products), specifications and prices directly with the production teams involved. The lead time was also established directly with these teams. The end result was a very short line of communication, quick decision making, and an end-product that very precisely met the customers' requirements. The shop floor teams in this case also chose when to work and, if they had finished a job after (for example) four days of the working week (one day ahead of schedule) they could choose to take the fifth day as additional paid leave. The teams were responsible for working with customers directly and accountable for their own success or failure. If they were late with an order, they were much more likely to work all hours to get the order prepared on time – because they had a direct relationship with the customer. In health care too, many organizations are making teams the primary point of contact for members of the public seeking health care.

7.3   BUSINESS PROCESSES OR INTERNAL EFFICIENCY

How good are the business processes (a term that may ring discordantly with those in public sector organizations but the principle of examining work processes applies equally there) of your organization and how short is the cycle time involved in producing products or delivering services? How efficiently and effectively does the organization function? Are meetings of an appropriate duration, content, style and level of productivity and innovation? Are team members clear about their objectives? Do the various departments communicate and work together effectively, minimizing unnecessary delays, communicating the correct information in a timely and helpful fashion? Is there good coordination and cooperation throughout the organization? Is the most efficient use being made of the resources of the organization – space, people, raw materials and so on?

In short, is the way that we produce products or deliver services as outstanding as it could possibly be? When our ancestors were trying to catch wildebeest on the savannah 200,000 years ago, getting the business processes right was a matter of eating or starving – of life and death. That meant they were constantly striving to improve their business processes to make the kill. No less, if we wish our organizations to be effective, we should concentrate on improving business processes. This refers to the quality of how we go about producing products or delivering services, and the speed with which the products or services are provided. Cycle time refers to how long it takes to produce the products or deliver the services. In one health care organization in which we worked the team of nurses proposed to bypass the normal procedure whereby patients contacted receptionists and arranged an appointment or a home visit with the first doctor available. The nurses proposed to take the calls (incidentally freeing up the receptionists to deal with patients face to face and manage the myriad of administrative tasks they had to deal with) and advise patients on whether they needed to see the doctor or the team nurse, whether they needed a home visit, whether they could treat themselves, or indeed whether they need not worry at all about their symptoms which would soon pass. Patients were still left with the final choice as to the route they chose. The end result was a rapid and dramatic reduction in the time for patients to receive diagnosis, advice or treatment and the number of visits by doctors to patients in their homes was reduced by 60 per cent. None of this was at the expense of patient satisfaction or patient care; on the contrary, patient satisfaction with the new scheme was extremely high – they were given more attention rather than less, and follow-up suggested they were receiving higher quality care as a result. Effectively, business processes were improved resulting in better quality and shorter cycle time.

How is team-based organizing contributing to better quality business processes and reducing cycle time in your organization and, again, how could TBW contribute yet further?

7.4   INNOVATION

Team-based organizations should be fountains of innovation – in products, services, production or service technologies, production processes, people-management practices and administrative procedures. After all, that is what teams are designed to do – integrate the diverse perspectives of individuals towards achieving a creative and effective new way forward. Therefore, a key indicator of the effectiveness of the innovative organization is the extent to which, as a consequence of team-based organizing, it is generating new products, processes or procedures. You can ask leaders the following questions:

• What changes in products has TBW introduced?
• What changes in production technology has TBW introduced?
• What changes in production techniques/procedures has TBW introduced?
• What changes in work organization has TBW introduced?
• What changes in human resource management has TBW introduced?

To what extent is TBW enabling innovation, both the development of ideas and their more effective implementation? Truly effective TBW should lead to more interteam cooperation, exchange and stimulation. In theory and in practice that leads to more innovation in products and services. There should be no shortage of ideas for new and improved products, services and ways of working in team-based organizations. W.L. Gore, a manufacturer of outdoor clothing (among many other things), is organized almost entirely in teams within organizational groupings of no more than 100 to 200 employees. Innovation is the means by which this company stands out as such an outstanding example to others over many years of operation. And innovations that can be applied and successfully exploited are truly valued within the organization.

Innovation evokes resistance and that is the principal reason why many good ideas for new products or services never reach the stage of being implemented. In team-based organizations, where people are working together to bring about change, and across teams and departments to resolve conflicts, implementing a good idea should be easier. There should be more power in the impetus for change (a whole team rather than one individual) and less resistance to it (the intergroup communication reduces distrust and rivalry). Another way of monitoring the contribution of TBW is therefore to assess whether resistance to change in the organization is generally decreasing. There is considerable evidence that change initiatives are more successful in organizations where team working is part of the change initiative or where TBW already exists.

EMPLOYEE LEARNING AND GROWTH

A subcomponent of innovation (in fact a major driver of innovation) to consider in evaluating the contribution of team-based organizing to organizational effectiveness is employee learning and growth. To what extent are employees developing their skills in the directions they wish for and in ways which enhance the organization's ability to meet its objectives? Skill development is likely to be strongly linked to employee motivation when employees feel the organization is investing in them, enabling them to do their jobs better and to learn from other team members. Indeed, one indicator of the effectiveness of team-based organizing is the extent to which team members learn skills, knowledge and abilities from other team members. Through the intense interaction in teams, members should learn new skills and develop knowledge that enhances both their individual and team functioning. This in turn leads to innovation.

Employee learning is all the more likely where good people management systems are in place, encouraging the identification of training needs and encouraging skill sharing. Such an environment will be challenging but not exhausting. Demands on employees will not exceed their ability (or perceived ability) to meet them. Where employees find themselves in positions in which demands exceed their resources, they are likely to feel stressed and anxious – precisely the conditions that inhibit learning. Moreover, they are likely to take time off on a frequent basis, express dissatisfaction and their intent to leave the organization, and finally to leave – taking their valuable skills and knowledge with them. One UK organization, the Defence Aviation Repair Agency (DARA), responded to an increasingly stressful and competitive environment by developing team-based working, and it has been so successful in this and in a consequent commitment to training that it has now spun out a completely new business in training aviation engineers.

To what extent therefore is team-based organizing contributing to employee skill development and growth and is team-based organizing leading to a reduction in absenteeism and employee turnover? In our experience of introducing team-based organizing, the most successful attempts are accompanied by a reduction in absenteeism and turnover and an increase in expressions of satisfaction. The best functioning teams exhibit lower levels of absenteeism and employee turnover than those that function less well. Moreover, our research data consistently show that in well-functioning teams, member stress levels are relatively low and members report high levels of learning from each other. To what extent has team-based organizing led to an increase in employee satisfaction and a decrease in employee stress? These questions can be answered by administering the simple measures described below (and included on the accompanying CD) to individual team members.

Score the job satisfaction questionnaire by adding the individual scores and dividing by the number of answers given (if all are answered this would be 16). Scores from 4.1 to 5 indicate moderate satisfaction and above 5 a high level of satisfaction. Average scores of 4 or below suggest major morale problems in an organization. Leaders should be aiming to achieve average satisfaction scores above 5 across the organization. Given the strong links between average employee satisfaction and company productivity, this target should be accorded a high priority.

To score the Psychological Health questionnaire, reverse the scores for items 2, 4, 6, 7, 9, 11, 13, 15, 17, 19, 21, 22, 25 ($1 = 5$, $2 = 4$, $3 = 3$, $4 = 2$, $5 = 1$). Then derive a total score. Scores of 60 or over indicate a high level of stress. Scores of 50 or less indicate a low level of stress. If a team member's score is over 60 and they are feeling generally under pressure, they may find it helpful to talk through their concerns with their family doctor or review their lifestyle with a qualified counsellor (in the United Kingdom the British Association of Counselling keeps a register of accredited counsellors).

Has the introduction of team-based organizing led to a reduction in absenteeism and employee turnover? In which areas of the organization are these reductions greatest and what can be learned from them about which team working practices are working best?

It is comfortable to review successes of team-based organizing in this way of course, but there are also potential threats to organizational effectiveness introduced by team-based organizing.

JOB SATISFACTION QUESTIONNAIRE

	Extremely dissatisfied	Very dissatisfied	Moderately dissatisfied	Not sure	Moderately satisfied	Very satisfied	Extremely satisfied
1 The physical working conditions	1	2	3	4	5	6	7
2 The freedom to choose your own method of working	1	2	3	4	5	6	7
3 Your fellow team members	1	2	3	4	5	6	7
4 The recognition you get for good work	1	2	3	4	5	6	7
5 Your immediate boss	1	2	3	4	5	6	7
6 The amount of responsibility you are given	1	2	3	4	5	6	7
7 Your rate of pay	1	2	3	4	5	6	7
8 The opportunity to use your ability	1	2	3	4	5	6	7
9 Relationships between management and workers in the organization	1	2	3	4	5	6	7
10 Your chance of promotion or progression within the company	1	2	3	4	5	6	7
11 The way your firm is managed	1	2	3	4	5	6	7
12 The attention paid to suggestions you make	1	2	3	4	5	6	7
13 Your hours of work	1	2	3	4	5	6	7
14 The amount of variety in your job	1	2	3	4	5	6	7
15 Your job security	1	2	3	4	5	6	7
16 The amount of training you receive	1	2	3	4	5	6	7

Adapted from Warr et al. (1979).

PSYCHOLOGICAL HEALTH QUESTIONNAIRE

How have you been feeling recently i.e., over the last four weeks?

	Not at all	Only occasionally	Quite often	Almost all of the time	All of the time
1 I have felt anxious	1	2	3	4	5
2 I have felt optimistic	1	2	3	4	5
3 I have felt depressed	1	2	3	4	5
4 I have felt positive	1	2	3	4	5
5 I have felt irritable	1	2	3	4	5
6 I have felt loving and warm to others	1	2	3	4	5
7 I have felt energetic	1	2	3	4	5
8 I have felt tearful	1	2	3	4	5
9 I have felt calm	1	2	3	4	5
10 I have felt unwell	1	2	3	4	5
11 I have felt happy	1	2	3	4	5
12 I have felt overwhelmed by everything	1	2	3	4	5
13 I have felt fit and healthy	1	2	3	4	5
14 I have had difficulty sleeping	1	2	3	4	5
15 I have felt excited	1	2	3	4	5
16 I have felt angry with others	1	2	3	4	5
17 I have felt enthusiastic	1	2	3	4	5
18 I have felt afraid	1	2	3	4	5
19 I have felt joyful	1	2	3	4	5
20 I have had lots of aches and pains	1	2	3	4	5
21 I have felt peaceful	1	2	3	4	5
22 I have felt at ease	1	2	3	4	5
23 I have felt like giving up	1	2	3	4	5
24 I have felt ill	1	2	3	4	5
25 I have felt relaxed	1	2	3	4	5

The most serious is the development of silos, at best indifferent to each other and at worst hostile. Symptoms of these problems are a clear indicator of the ineffectiveness of team-based organizing in your organization.

7.5 INTERGROUP RELATIONS

In the last two chapters we have discussed issues of intergroup relationships on a number of occasions and suggested that effective team-based organizing is characterized by levels of intergroup conflict and suspicion lower than those that existed prior to the change. However, organizations that have simply introduced teams, without addressing issues of intergroup relations, may see an increase in intergroup conflict rather than a decrease. Cohesive teams are more likely to be suspicious of, and competitive with, other teams in the organization. In team-based organizing, as much effort is put into building relationships *across* teams as into developing relationships *within* teams. This is crucial to understanding that team-based organizing is much more than simply about developing teamwork.

The consequences of improving interteam, interdepartmental, interprofessional, and cross-functional working should be measurable in relation to all the dimensions of effectiveness described above (goal achievement, business processes, customer satisfaction, employee learning, and innovation). But also it should be clear that intergroup relationships are themselves improving with evidence of less conflict and more cooperation between teams, groups, departments and professionals. The silos should have been removed to reveal areas where groups can explore and build together. The following Intergroup Relations questionnaire, developed by Andreas Richter at Aston Business School, can be used to assess interteam or interdepartmental cooperation and conflict:

In general, when you interact with members of the other team:

Task conflict

1 How frequently do you have *conflicts about ideas* with members of the other team?

2 How frequently do you have *disagreements* with members of the other team about a *task/project* you are working on?

3 How frequently do you have *differences of opinion* about a *task/project* with members of the other team?

4 How frequently do you have *disagreements* with members of the other team *about work-related viewpoints*?

5 How frequently do you have *animated discussions* about *differences of opinion* with members of the other team?

Relationship conflict

6 How much *friction* is there with members of the other team?

7 How much *relationship tension* do you have with members of the other team?

8 How often does interaction with members of the other team produce *anger*?

9 How much *emotional conflict* do you have with members of the other team?

10 How often are you *frustrated* after interacting with members of the other team?

Process conflict

11 How often do you have *disagreements* with members of the other team about *'who should do what'*?

12 How much *conflict about task responsibilities* do you have with members of the other team?

13 How often do you have *disagreements about resource allocation* with members of the other team?

14 There is agreement between my group and the other group.

15 The other group withholds information necessary for the attainment of our group tasks.

16 The relationship between my group and the other group is harmonious in attaining the overall organizational goal.

17 There is lack of mutual assistance between my group and the other group.

18 There is cooperation between my group and the other group.

19 The other group creates problems for my group.

Respondents can score most items on a scale from 1 (almost never), 2 (occasionally), 3 (usually), 4 (frequently), to 5 (almost all the time). For items 6, 7, 9 and 12 score items on a scale from 1 (almost none), 2 (a small amount), 3 (a moderate amount), 4 (a high amount), 5 (a very high amount). High scores (above an average of 2) in relation to process or relationship conflict indicate real problems that should be addressed. Moderate scores in relation to task conflict (2 to 3) are generally an indication of an appropriate level of task-related conflict.

7.6 RELATIONSHIPS BETWEEN TEAMS AND ORGANIZATIONS

Another dimension that can be used to consider the effectiveness of team-based organizing is to consider the extent to which relationships between teams and the organization have shifted – especially among front-line staff – from the old command and control cultures.

If teams are working well, they should be fountains of innovative ideas and practices. Team members should also be developing an awareness of the contribution their work can make to the overall goals of the organization, both because of their increasing involvement in decision making and contact with customers and the reduced layers of hierarchy that were formerly barriers to communication and speedy decision making. In team-based organizations, teams are therefore likely to rely appropriately rather than unquestioningly on organizational directions – where team members see paradoxes or inconsistencies in organizational policies, they are likely to question senior managers about them rather than grumbling mutinously among themselves. They are likely to question rather than accept organizational incompetence and inadequacies and challenge inappropriate ways of doing things, however orthodox or whether sanctioned by senior managers. Such ways of working should be encouraged by senior managers as a sign of the health of team-based organizing rather than as an indication of the organization getting out of control or of a failure of leadership. The uncertainty created by questioning and the ambiguity developed by preparedness of teams to challenge the status quo are sources of innovation and development and you should perceive them as such. Of course the organization has a job to get on with and endless debates about arcane issues of procedure would be destructive, but in a team-based organization, the shared alignment of all teams and their members around organizational goals, and a climate of reflexivity, together ensure the challenges and questioning lead to better achievement of goals.

7.7 LONG-TERM REVIEW

Your organization's success in the application of TBW depends on the continual review of, and reflection on, your TBW processes and strategies, and subsequent adaptation and development of your TBW objectives. This final stage therefore initiates a continuing process to review your organization's functioning in relation to TBW, to ensure that TBW remains appropriate for your needs and that it continues to contribute to your organization's effectiveness.

How can senior managers and the change manager best ensure the long-term success of TBW? The following are key strategies, which with regular monitoring can contribute to that long-term effectiveness:

- Ensure the top management team provides a model of effective teamworking.
- Ensure there are reviews of TBW between team leaders and top management in which team processes and organization hindrances and helps are discussed.
- Reflect on the need for new teams in the organization, as well as the need to disband existing teams that have run their course.
- Benchmark best practice against other organizations which have implemented TBW, especially those with a reputation for getting TBW right. Use both national and international organizations and encourage organization visits by team leaders to these best practice organizations.
- Continuously learn from teams and their members about effective and ineffective elements of TBW. Each organization is unique and must learn for itself which approaches are most effective, e.g. in relation to reward systems for teams or systems to ensure good cross-team communication.
- Regularly examine organization culture, structure and support systems to ensure they are consistent with, and supportive of, TBW. This can be achieved by regularly repeating Stage One of the TBW process – in effect, by treating TBW as a cyclical rather than a linear process.

- Regularly take time out to review organization objectives and organization processes. Explore how TBW can be developed to ensure that your objectives are clear and appropriate, that your strategies are effective and carefully thought through, and that your processes (decision making, communication, participation, and support for innovation) enable the implementation of strategies and achievement of objectives.

TBW involves deep, wide and pervasive changes within organizations. The journey is tough: there is much resistance to the changes and there are many setbacks. But the advantages are huge in comparison with other organization changes. As an organization or as the change manager, you will need to be courageous in the face of conflict, persistent in managing resistance and optimistic even during times of failure and difficulty.

7.8   BEYOND TEAM-BASED ORGANIZING

This book and accompanying CD are designed to enable organizations to develop a way of organizing that can produce effectiveness, innovation, employee growth and well-being, efficient business processes and satisfied customers. But the model can be taken further and, as we explore new organizational forms in our society, team-based organizing can also stretch its boundaries. Joint ventures, mergers, acquisitions, interorganizational working and organizations without boudaries offer new challenges to our concepts of a work community. How can we get two companies in the oil and gas industry to cooperate in making a new undersea drill that neither could make alone? How can we enable health service organizations, social service organizations and educational organizations to collaborate effectively in the delivery of services to promote the health and well-being of whole communities? How can we closely involve customers in the design and production process of a new car so that it truly meets their needs? One way to answer all these questions is to extend the model of team-based organizing so that it spans organically outside and across organizational boundaries. This is happening in relation to each of these areas. Oil and gas companies are forming joint venture teams that become new (albeit temporary) team-based organizations themselves. Health and social services are blurring the boundaries of their organizations to create more and more permanent teams made up of members from both sectors. Customers are joining design and production teams in many industries as full team members to ensure the product meets their needs rather than what the designers and production teams imagine are their needs. Patients are joining health care teams as advisors, as influential members and as advocates to ensure that services meet their needs.

Team-based organizing is changing as the demands of our changing environment illustrate the need for new ways of organizing human work communities. But the basis for all of this remains the devolution of responsibility to groups of people (in whatever organizations) working together to achieve shared goals in ways that maximize the value of their knowledge, skills and abilities. And they themselves are developing these new organizational forms that are enabling us to discover and develop our future. And that is the value of team-based organizing – that it puts into the hands of all of those in the organization the ability and responsibility to bring about the changes they feel are necessary to achieve their goals. It is so successful because it is the way of working we evolved over hundreds of thousands of years. It is how we caught wildebeest on the savannah, built our hospitals, educated our young in school systems, and explored both our genetic structure and our solar system. The challenge is to adapt modern large organizations to this way of working to fully benefit from the synergistic strength and adaptability that teamworking has always given us.

REFERENCES AND FURTHER READING

Hackman, J.R. (2002). *Leading Teams: Setting the Stage for Great Performances.* Cambridge, MA: Harvard Business School Press.

Heron, J. (1989). *The Facilitator's Handbook.* London: Kogan Page.

Kaplan, R.S. and Norton, D.P. (1998). Putting the balanced scorecard to work. *Harvard Business Review,* September/October: 134–47.

Macy, B.A. and Izumi, H. (1993). Organizational change, design and work innovation: A meta-analysis of 131 North American field studies, 1961–1991. *Research in Organizational Change and Development,* 7: 235–313.

McGill, I. and Beatty, L. (1992). *Action Learning: A Practitioner's Guide.* London: Kogan Page.

Patterson, M.G., West, M.A., Lawthom, R.L., & Nickell, S. (1997). People management and business performance. London: Institute for Personnel and Development.

Tjosvold, D. (1990). *Team Organization: An Enduring Competitive Advantage.* Chichester, UK: Wiley.

Warr, P.B., Cook, J., & Wall, T.D. (1979). Scales for the measurement of some work attitudes and aspects of psychological well-being. *Journal of Occupational Psychology,* 52: 129–48.

Weinstein, K. (1995). *Action Learning: A Journey in Discovery and Development.* London: HarperCollins.

West, M.A., (1994). *Effective Teamwork.* Oxford: Blackwell.

West, M.A. (ed.) (1996). *Handbook of Work Group Psychology.* Chichester, UK: Wiley.

West, M.A., Tjosvold, D., & Smith, K.G. (eds.) (2003). *International Handbook of Organizational Teamwork and Cooperative Working.* Chichester, UK: Wiley.

INDEX